# The Silent Truth....

By Ashley April

2012

Revised edition  February 2012

Copyright © 2012 by Ashley April
Photos by Ashley April
Poems by Dwight

All rights reserved

No part of this book may be used unless the author gives permission.
This book and the material that it contains is not to be reproduced in any way.
In addition, this book is for educational and inspirational reading purposes.
For any inquiries contact LuLu.com Raleigh, NC
www.lulu.com


Published in the United States of America.

978-1-257-74270-7

## Dedication

This is a story that my very best and closest friend inspired me to write. I would never have written this book, if he had not encouraged me. He has opened my eyes, to see how far I have come over the last twenty years. I would like to dedicate this book to all the people that have touched my life. Given me encouragement, support and love.

I am blessed to have three best friends, and I want to thank each of you. For your love and support throughout my struggles. Your unconditional love that you give to me each and every day. Thank you for the laughter and tears we have shared. Thank you, I will be forever in your debt.

I want to thank my mother and my grandmother. For your undying love and support. I appreciate everything that you both have done for me and continue to give me. I am truly sorry for the difficult times I have put you both through.

Thank you to my one and only little brother. For always being there when I needed you most. I really think that you were born first. You have taken on the "big" brother roll. I am so proud of you and I am so proud to be your sissy. I love you!

Thank you to my father, for never ever being disappointed in me. For your unconditional love that you gave to me in the short time you were here on earth.

And finally to my boys, my **guardian angels.** I did it all for you both. You were my saving grace. You were my only strength I carried for a very long time. My whole life has been for you. And I love you both very very much!

I hope that you are inspired by the words you are about to read. I hope that it touches your life and opens your eyes as well. Be thankful for the gifts you have. Not the material ones...the gift of life, the gift of family, the gift of friends, the gift of laughter and humor, the gift of having hopes n dreams, hugs n kisses, smiles n LOVE...You have many gifts and we all take them for granted.

Remember...every day that goes by is one that you will never get back...

My cry's go out,
no one hears them.
His hands of anger,
I always fear them.
Close my eyes,
tremble and shake.
What have I done,
these bones he breaks.
The words of love fills my ears,
can never stop the rushing tears.
For the two I will be strong.
Didn't want to be here this long.
No where to go,
no where to run. Never will I leave my
sons. Courage in me I have to make,
my will not given for him to break.
Close my eyes,
peace is near.
Never again him I fear!


Eyes of anger look right through me,
bleeding heart thought you knew me.
You lash out at me, call me names,
always saying I was to blame!
Too busy to see I was hurting too,
the pain I feel I thought you had a clue!
Blinded by your one way truth,
ignoring my pain is nothing new.
Now you want me more than ever!
Saying life was never better!
If only you could of seen all this before,
I may have not walked out the door!

# *The Silent Truth...*

## This is my story...

    My parents were married for about eight years or so. I have a few good memories, memories of the four of us being a family. We did holidays with my grandparents and we spent time with our uncles. I recall going on vacations, the four of us, Niagra Falls and Six Gun City. I remember my parents fighting quite a bit, when I was young. They were divorced when I was about nine years old. My mother had custody of my brother and I. We would spend time at my dad's house on the weekends. But there came a point when my brother wanted to stay with my dad full time, as every boy his age would want. So he went to live with him. I was a bit envious of that, I really missed having my father around every night. For a long time it was just mom and I. We didn't spend a lot of time together. She was a single mom, and worked a lot of hours. She did what she could to make ends meet. My dad was a hard worker too. He had two businesses going on. He owned a garage, employed one mechanic besides himself. He also had a tow truck that was part of that business. My uncle owned the gas pumps and my dad ran the mechanical side. In addition, my dad logged with another uncle, splitting and delivering wood for heating in the Vermont winters.

    My mother did take time out for us when she could, I remember her taking us on trips. She took me to New York City on a bus tour. We went to the Statue of Liberty, we saw the Empire State Building, and the King Tut exhibit at the Metropolitan Museum of Art. A good friend of hers lived in Philadelphia, she took me there for a visit as well, only this time she drove us. Later on, that friend moved to Delaware and all three of us went on a trip to visit her. My mom wasn't afraid to go any where and she tried her best to show us the world, or what was in her grasp. Traveling was fun, she made it fun. I don't recall my brother going with us very often, more than likely he just wanted to be with our dad. She was able to get tickets one time for the Montreal Expos, we went to Canada for a weekend to see a professional baseball game. A few years later my grandparents were taking a trip to the mid west. They were driving some family back home to South Dakota. I was able to go on that trip with them, it was something that is to be treasured. I saw so many things and learned a lot about the US. The highlight of this trip was seeing Mount Rushmore.

My mother was married for a second time, but it was a short lived marriage. He showed his true colors after they said their vows. She went through a lot with him. But she broke away and finally met a man that ended up being married to her for more than twenty years.

My dad found a nice woman, though they never married, you could just tell they were meant to be. They were good for each other, balanced each other and just clicked. They laughed a lot and that was really nice to see. After years of being unhappy, I enjoyed seeing my dad's life have joy in it.

So we had separate families. My parents weren't Ozzie n Harriet. I looked at my friend's parents with such envy at times. Wondering what it would be like to have my parents still be married to each other and live under the same roof. I guess that is every kid's dream, that comes from a broken home. Something that most kids have, but take it for granted. I secretly told myself, when I had kids, I wasn't going to allow them to be brought up in a broken home. I wanted something different for them. Thinking that it was the way it should be. The naïve thoughts of kid...

At 16 I was very quiet and stepped back from the crowd. I had a boyfriend that was older. My mother didn't approve of course. Hind sight, I wish she had forbidden it. But I think she knew there would be resentment. For that I thank her. I probably would've done it anyways. After being together for awhile, I began gaining weight. I had always struggled with it all my life. But being naive - I didn't think...I was actually eating for two. At eight months pregnant, I realized something wasn't right. I was sick all the time, vomiting at the drop of a hat and then wanting to eat again because I was so hungry.

I finally sat down and talked to my mother. I had been in such denial. I was indeed pregnant and going to be a mother. I was faced with grown up decisions that I was in no way ready to accept. In the tenth grade, you have absolutely no clue. No clue about anything let alone being a mother. She forced those grown up things onto me right away. She made me go tell my father. That was the hardest conversation I had ever rehearsed in my mind. Telling my father that he was going to be a grandpa, when I myself was still his little girl. I hated the thought of disappointing him. He took it like a trooper. He never made me feel like I had disappointed him. I then, made the decision to quit school. Against everyone's wishes. I was hell bent, that I would go back. But no one believed me...

After finally going to the doctor, he discovered that my baby was breech. I was so far along; there was no time to turn him. So here I go, never having had surgery before. A c-section was scheduled. Scared out of my mind, I didn't know what to do.

The Friday before surgery was to be performed. I felt really sick. My back hurt. I was so uncomfortable. I laid around in bed all day, just hoping that I would feel better. Little did I know,

I was in labor. My mother and grandmother had traveled out of state for the day. They went to tell my grandfather that I was pregnant. He had been in the hospital out of state, for a few months at that time. Towards that evening I decided that a hot shower may help me out. In the process of getting in the shower, my water broke. I didn't know that's what it was. I thought my bladder had just let go. Then my back got worse! Getting more scared, I called my boyfriend. I was rushed to the hospital. Fear of the unknown set in. All I could do was cry. It was all a flash. My boyfriend was there, he took me to the hospital. But I went through the rest all by myself. I was left there at the hospital to face the scariest thing I had ever encountered up to that pointin my life. Alone.

I had a baby boy. He was the cutest baby I had ever seen. He looked just like the Gerber baby on television and in the magazine ads. I was so proud of that little bundle. He was pretty precious. I couldn't believe that I had brought that wonderful creature into the world.

After what seemed to be a long healing process from surgery, long and difficult. I had an infection in my incision. They had to reopen it up for it to heal correctly. I remember thinking that the labor I was in in the previous few days, was nothing compared to the pain of this infection. I was in the hospital for a week, rather than a few days. I was scared. The nurses that I was blessed to have, were like mothers to me. I learned so much from them about taking care of myself and my newborn. One nurse in particular took a lot of time with me. She would come and sit with me when I fed my son. She would bring me books to read. She was full of all kinds of advice. Reality of motherhood was settling in.

It wasn't glamorous, it wasn't fun. At 16, you really have no idea what a big responsibility you have. Even though it's there and "in your face". Waking up at all hours of the night, warming up a bottle and changing a diaper. I had a lot of help from my gram and my mother. I sure couldn't have done it without either of them.

Being a mother was very difficult but when I looked at him sleeping, I was amazed! I was truly blessed. Some people weren't as lucky having a healthy baby and a family that still loved them. I was never dis – owned by any of them. I was very thankful for that, but still being a teenager, I didn't show my appreciation.

Before my son was born, my son's father gave me a ring. I thought at the time, that was what I wanted. Everyone around me told me it would never work... "You won't get married..." I had it set in my mind that I was going to make it. He was there a little bit after the childbirth. I continued living with my mother and her new husband. I would stay quite often at my grandparents as well.

After I had really healed from my c-section and was feeling better. Mom offered to watch my son so we could go out to the movies. I was really looking forward to it. I had one friend that was always around for me. She got us out of the house and came to visit often. She helped keep me sane. I missed going out on dates though, so it was something I was excited about. We went, enjoyed dinner and a movie. But before taking me home, he pulled over and said he wanted to talk. Well, that wasn't what he had in mind. It was dark and secluded. I was a bit nervous and not comfortable. I asked him to just take me home. He persisted. I had all ready decided that I wasn't going to have sex again for a very long time. The reality of being a teen mom was great birth control. He knew how I felt about it, and he didn't respect that. He had "needs" and that was all that mattered. He wouldn't take no for an answer. He made me do things that I didn't want to do.

The next day he came to my house to see us and I met him at the door. I wouldn't let him in. He couldn't figure out why. Well, I let him know why...I told him that there was a word for what he had done. It was called RAPE – I told him I didn't ever want to see him again. He finally respected my wishes and completely walked away, never to look back. So there it was, it was my son & I against the world. That was when I was hell bent on graduating high school!

My grandmother offered to watch my son while I went back to school. I ended up going back in what would've been my senior year. I crammed what everyone thought was too many classes into my schedule. I was busy and stressed with a lot of pressure. My grandmother saved me! She helped me like no other. I stayed with my grandparents during the week and at my mom's on the weekends. My grandmother put up with a lot from me and having my son all the time. I owe her so much. I could not have done it without her.

My work load at school was very hectic. Half way through the year I was realizing everyone around me was wrong. I could do this. I was passing my classes. I knew I was going to do it. I was going to make it. I was walking to and from the bus stop, about half a mile away and losing weight. The only time I didn't walk was in a snow storm. My dad was the road commissioner and he would pick me up in the big truck when he was out plowing. That was pretty darn cool! He saw how diligent I was at going to school and what it meant to me to finish.

Back when I was in the ninth grade, I briefly had a boyfriend at school. We didn't really do much but hold hands and he walked me to class. We kissed on the bleachers at the school dances and that was about as exciting as it got. It didn't last very long. He went into the navy after graduating. It was a long time before I ever heard from him again. Somehow he got a hold of me when I was a senior. We wrote, we talked on the phone. We caught up on what had been going on with each other. He was coming home in Feb for some scheduled leave. He was home for two weeks. While he was here he gave me a diamond ring. He wanted to marry me. So I said yes. Looking back now, I think that I was in love with being in love. So I started planning a small summer wedding, for after graduation. I was excited. I was seeing it as a way to get away from where I grew up. And hopefully give my son a better life.

In June 1989, I graduated from high school with MY class. I was given an achievement award for my hard work. I made up two years in one and I did what I set out to do! I got my diploma. I was so proud of myself. I felt awesome!

As the big day approached, I was having mixed feelings about getting married. His parents didn't approve because I was a teen mom. The odds were stacking up against us. He was able to be home for my graduation. He told me that he was getting out of the navy, which was news to me. He was expecting me to live with him at his grandparent's farm / bed & breakfast. Not really the life I was dreaming of. When we started making plans for our life, he was going to be stationed in Guam. Taking me out of this country, we were going to see the world. That prospect was very appealing to me. But one day, just a few days from the wedding day, he showed me a side of him that was a bit controlling. Without even thinking, in that instant, I called off the wedding. That was it. I was moving on. Not regretting it for a moment.

So when I got rid of the second guy in my life. I had to figure out what I was going to do with the rest of my life, or at least the immediate future. Diploma in hand, now what do I do? I got a job as a cashier. Certainly nothing glamorous, not making much money at all. But I went to work every day.

As that summer moved on, riding around with my friends & my son (he went everywhere with me – I didn't want to be one of those moms that goes out and ditches her kid off to Grammy). Riding around we met up with a friend of my friend that was with me. She hooked us up. He knew I had a kid; she made that clear to him right off the bat. He still wanted to see me, so we started dating. I really liked him. I thought he might be the one. He had accepted me, my son, and the whole package. So my third engagement ring, I thought maybe number three is my lucky number. So we took the plunge. That December after graduating, we were married. Yes it was quick. I truly thought this was the man I would be with forever. We were young, 18 and 20.

We were married for less than a month and I found out that I was pregnant. Everyone was excited. I was too, for a little while. Then I got scared. I felt trapped. I shouldn't of, but I did. It was a rough pregnancy. I was sick, I was tired and I was extremely moody. I was not enjoying being pregnant at all. I was getting excited for the actual birth though. I was not having a c-section this time. I was really going to experience child birth. I ended up having to be induced. I was in labor all day, once again. Hard labor for about six hours. I felt like a pin cushion. They finally gave me something to ease the pain for awhile so I could rest before pushing. I was so grateful for that drug! It dulled the pain until I was dilated enough to push. I was so excited to hopefully have a girl; the nurse had a pink bed all set up. My mother even thought it would be a girl; just by the way I was carrying. As soon as I pushed that last time, and the baby arrived. My husband says "get that pink out." It's a boy! I was a little let down, but when he was laid on me, I saw how precious he was and I forgot all about it.

His brother loved him from the very start. I loved to watch them together. They played and giggled, I enjoyed being with them so much. When I was with them, I was wrapped up in those moments, thinking there was no better reward than being a mother. It was two things that I had accomplished. I brought them into this world. I was so proud of my beautiful boys.

Well life went on. I had left the work force early on in my pregnancy, and regretted it. But I wanted to be home and take care of my boys. We were struggling to make ends meet. I took action and got us into low income housing. It was more affordable. Soon after, my husband was laid off. He started blaming me for being in that situation, because I had left my job. He was laid off and didn't work for years. He gained weight. Got bossy. Made me feel like it was my entire fault that we were in the predicament that we were in. He got violent often. He was becoming a very angry person and difficult to live with. Almost, as if he were a living time bomb.

About a year or so after he was laid off, I found a part time job as a cashier. It was OK. It helped get me out and it was a little bit of money. Then I had a scare. I thought I was pregnant. I was upset for days, contemplating what I was going to do. I was on the pill and so angry and scared. Then I got my period. Relief! I wasn't about to bring into the world another baby. Not in the situation I was presently in. No way, that wasn't fair. So I went to the doctor. We discussed my options. I decided to get my tubes tied, but I had to wait until I was 21. As soon as I was able to, I had the surgery.

When they had me opened, they ran some routine tests. They discovered that I had endometriosis. I hadn't known because I was all ready taking one of the treatments, I was on the pill. Well after recovering from surgery, I just wasn't feeling myself. Not well at all. I still had my period. So I thought that it was normal. Until I was hunched over in excruciating pain - every minute of my period. Then when I started passing blood clots, I went back to the doctor. He gave me Tylenol with codeine, so when I was having my period, I was worthless. Drained, tired, it was taking its toll on me. I suffered for months. I had no compassion from my husband. He had alienated my family, so I hardly saw them. The friend that got us together, he pushed away as well. She was way too opinionated for me to be around, in his eyes. So all I had was his family. For the most part they made me feel like family.

My husband had made friends with a neighbor who raced at the local track. They became good friends and he was asked to join the pit crew. That was all good; it got him out, but a little too much. As he was hanging out with these people, there was a girl that hung out with them. She was over 20 and still a virgin. There was much talk about her. I felt very insecure about it. Because in my husband's eyes, I was no longer attractive. I had gained weight, just as he had. I had no self esteem.

Well one weekend, they decided that they were going to expand to another race track. They were going to NY. I will never forget this day. I wasn't even asked to go. There was a group of people going over there too. There happened to be no room in the car hauler for my husband, so he was riding along with the group in a van. Who was driving that van? THE VIRGIN. All that morning I was in horrible pain with my period. I needed medication badly. He was still planning on going. So he asked his sister to come over and watch the boys while I ran down to the pharmacy. Never offering to go for me, never asked someone to pick them up for me. I had to muster on some clothes and go myself. I was crushed! Was I not worth a few minutes of someone's time? I came back from getting my medication refilled and took them. I laid the boys down for a nap and I snuggled in bed with them and slept too. Later that day I passed the biggest blood clot ever and I was scared to death.

When he got home that night, all I heard about was how much fun he had had. What the "virgin" had said and on and on he went. I felt like dying. I felt horrible not only physically, but emotionally. He never even asked how I was feeling either.

That following Monday I went back to the doctor. I made the decision to have a complete hysterectomy. I just couldn't deal with the pain any longer. At least one pain could be eliminated. By this time, surgery felt like an old pair of jeans – easy to get into. So it was scheduled and it was all taken out. While they were in there this time, they discovered that I had two cysts the size of a grapefruit. It explained a lot. Just in a span of six months they had grown. At less than 22 years old I was put right into menopause.

I took hormone replacements and finally started feeling better. I really reflected back on what had happened, when I was laying there in that hospital bed. I was so grateful for having been a teen mom. Otherwise, I wouldn't have my kids...

After years my husband finally found a job. He went from no work to working sixty hours a week. He was too tired to fight with me, so things started feeling better. We moved out of low income housing and moved to another town. Life was getting better. The boys were in school. I had a few hours to myself each day and then I started to get bored. I found a job as a cashier, once again. I worked the four to midnight shifts and I loved it. I could walk to work. My sister in law watched the boys until my husband got out of work. It was going really well until I had a little crush on this customer that came in the store all the time. My husband started getting jealous and started showing up at work and just stood around the store, watching me. I started to see a side of him that scared me. I was enjoying going to work because it got me away from him. This guy I had a crush on was older, very nice to me. Called me beautiful, he was just very sweet to me. I knew nothing would ever come of it; he just made me feel good. There was no affair or anything. Just a very nice guy that made me feel good for the few minutes I saw him. I was forced to quit that job.

I found a job housekeeping part time at a bed & breakfast in town. I got great tips and I liked it. I then found a job at a nursing home shortly after and it was in walking distance and it was a full time position. Nothing glamorous, but it was a good job for the amount of education I had. I loved the elderly; it was rewarding being around them. By that time both of the boys were in school full time. So it was good, I worked an early shift 7am-3pm. I was there for quite awhile. I was losing weight once again, because of all the walking.

We decided it was time for a home of our own. We bought a mobile home in a park on the other end of town. We had just one car, so I was stuck walking to and from work. I caught a ride once in awhile, but for the most part I hoofed it. I had no choice but to put the boys into daycare after school at that point in time. It worked OK; it was between work and home. Work was about two miles away. By the time the kids and I got home it would be about five o'clock. I was so exhausted. Nights that supper wasn't ready and on the table when my husband got home, there was an issue. He had become barbaric. Making me wait on him hand and foot. I was expected to be wife, mother, and housekeeper (at home and at work) and continue to be the Energizer bunny.

My husband had never been able to have a dog where he grew up. So over the years any chance that he got (which he made those chances) he would bring home a dog. All the places we lived, dogs were not permitted. So we were breaking the rules and had to hide it. Somehow, in his mind, he seemed to think that the rules didn't apply to him. So when we got into our own home, he took it upon himself to get a dog. The boys were still pretty little and this was a big dog. Playing with the boys, one day, he nipped one of them in the face. There were no physical injuries, but instead of figuring out what happened, so as to prevent it in the future, he jumped to conclusions. Told me to grab the gun out of the closet and we took the dog for a ride. We went down a secluded road and pulled over. Barking orders at me to get out of the car and hold the dog. Tears taking hold of me, he made me hold the dog still while he put the gun barrel to its head. He shot that dog right there and thought that it was kosher. Well it wasn't, the boys were in the back seat of the car. I had time before I stepped out of the car, to instruct them to stay buckled up and not to move. I didn't want them seeing what their father had in store for this dog's fate. But they knew, they sat there and cried. It was a sight that broke my heart in two. Not just for the boys, but that innocent dog that had met his fate that day. That man that I had married, had rescued that dog. And without batting an eyelash, took his life. I couldn't believe what that monster of a man had done. I couldn't believe what a cold hearted soul he had become. That should have been an event that opened my eyes. But I was blinded by the fact that I was married to him and I thought that because I had said those vows, I had to stick it out. That day changed me, as it should. It hit me in my very core. I saw a side of that man that I didn't like, and it made the eggshells I walked on daily, turn to shards of glass.

One year when we got our tax refund, he bought a lifted truck. Well that was HIS toy. But I didn't care, I got the car. So I felt somewhat better. A win – win situation… I was able to drive to work and pick up my boys.

After moving into our home, I became friends with a girl I worked with. She lived in the same park. We'd hang out and I really liked her. She was at my house a lot. She very rarely had her husband or son with her. Which I thought was odd…

She called us one night, all in a panic. She needed my husband's help; there was a pipe under her kitchen sink that had busted. I rushed him out the door with a wrench in hand. He was gone for hours. I thought, "That poor girl…where is her husband?" well mine came strolling in well after midnight. He told me he fixed the pipe and what an ordeal it was. I commended him for doing the deed and losing some sleep because of it. Over the next few weeks he would stop and see how the job he had done was holding up. At dinner he would tell us little tid bits of things that he had learned about my "friend". They "locked" their son in his room, her husband was hitting her and she was protecting her son by locking him up…so I questioned her. She cried and cried. I felt so bad for the girl. So I encouraged my husband to check on her more and more. I was worried about her.

One day at work there was a group of LNA's standing around talking and I heard my name. I smiled at them when I walked by. A few minutes later one of my co workers cornered me in the locker room. She told me that my "friend" is saying that she is having an affair with my husband. Denial was first and foremost. So I called my husband and he came over at my lunch break. I asked him point blank if it was true. He just stared out in space. As the tears began to fall, I felt sick to my stomach. Not speaking a word, he told me everything. He finally opened his mouth and said "yes." My world had come to an end. I was crushed beyond belief. Betrayed by my husband AND my supposed best friend. A friend that I finally had, someone that I trusted and confided in. I found it very difficult to trust anyone from that day on.

Totally in a daze, hearing whispers, I finished out my day. I went home. Just wanting to be with my kids and see their innocent faces and hold them close. They were the ones that counted. I don't really remember much of that night, but I do remember this...I went to my "friend's" place and my husband was there. I walked in and said "you have a choice." He chose me. She had started stalking him at work. She made him think that she was pregnant with his baby. He had been "running scared" – I think that he was kind of relieved that it was all out in the open now. This woman wanted my life. My husband, my kids, my home! Well, that was it! That night, she no longer existed. I shut down. I bottled it up. Moved on and didn't talk about it. Yes, I even continued to work there...

That summer I was going to have issues paying for day care, it was going to soak up most of my paycheck. My husband's sister offered to watch my boys at our place for the summer. I thought, great, and we jumped on that offer. The boys loved it. They could sleep in and play with the neighbor kids.

One day not too long after summer started. I was startled by a phone call at work, "your house is on fire!!" I was so upset; one of my co workers drove me there. All I could think of was my kids. When we arrived I frantically looked for them. Crying and so upset, finally seeing their faces, we clung to each other for a very long spell. We watched the firemen clean up the hoses and all that was left there standing was a shell. Not much to salvage at all.

In a little over a month's time, I had my husband cheat on me, lost my "best friend" and now what I had called home. I was thankful for my boys and my health. All I had materialistically was my car and a few belongings that didn't burn. One item that had survived amazingly enough, was a cedar chest that my father had built for me one Christmas. I treasure that! It was in our living room with the television on it. The TV had melted down but the chest hadn't been damaged!

So...we were homeless. We had many offers and much help. I was very grateful for what I did have. Between the Red Cross and our home owner's insurance, we got through it.

My brother came to be with me and gave me comfort that evening. He's younger than me, but he made it feel like he was the older one taking care of his baby sister. It was a great feeling, having him close by. He was a source of support and strength. He was the one person that my husband allowed to stay a part of my life. He liked my brother and considered him a friend, otherwise he would have been alienated too.

My husband decided that we would take the money and re-establish ourselves in a warmer climate. He was moving us to South Carolina, near some family of his. I was terrified. Taken away from the home state I had grown up in, Vermont. Taken away 1200 miles to where I knew no one. Reluctantly, I picked up and carried on. The way an obedient wife should. Packing up what little we had, into a small trailer in tow with the lifted truck, that I wasn't so sure would make it 1200 miles and my little car. We purchased cb radios so we could communicate on the road. We set out on an adventure of a life time. So my husband thought. In my mind, I was just following.

It was a hot and muggy day. We traveled as far as PA that first day. Leaving the next morning the heat was worse than the day before. No a/c in either vehicle, we were very uncomfortable. We ran into rain and made the drive even worse, being forced to keep the windows rolled up. It was torrential down pour; the grass on the side of the highway was pushed over by the wind. It looked as if a helicopter was landing on it. I was very scared, trying to be strong for my kids; I put up a good front. I had never driven in such conditions.

All we owned was in those vehicles; I didn't want to lose more. That night we stopped in North Carolina. We watched the news and the weather that we had gone through had produced tornadoes. At the precise time we were on that route, going through that town. That was a tornado that went across that highway, just behind us. We had barely missed it. I just cried. All I could think of was, "what if..." I had my babies and what was left of my life and that came close to being gone with the wind. At that point, I was homesick. I wanted nothing more than to be home in my bed, snuggled up with my two boys. Then reality set in. I have no home. I have no bed. All I had was my strength. And I was losing that, fast.

We got up and going the next morning, pressing onward. Where I found the strength is beyond me. A promise of a better life was on the horizon. No more shoveling snow. No more cold weather. We had watched the news before leaving the motel. There was a threat of a hurricane coming; I think it was called Bertha. We contemplated staying in NC, more inland until it was over. But the excitement of it to my husband, was going through it. So we pressed on one more day. We were finally on the last leg of our journey there. The worst of the traffic was yet to come. We were just "country-folk" living in a state that only had two lane highways. Going through Charlotte, where there are four and six lanes of traffic. We were totally out of our element. But we got through it. We made it to the last route, which would take us all the way to Ladson, SC. I-26, it was beautiful. It reminded me of what I was used to. Two lane highway, that for a good part of it was lined with trees. The day was gorgeous. It was sunny and very warm. I couldn't see how there could be bad weather coming.

We arrived late in the afternoon. We were greeted with open arms. I felt at ease, surprisingly. We had been there a few hours and as we were unpacking some clothes, the boys discovered a horrible thing that we didn't have back home. Two years prior they had been stung by a hive of bees and rushed to the hospital. The memories of that were still quite fresh. While we were handing them items from the car, teddy bears n blankies, they stood there on the lawn, right on top of a fire ant mound. The screams to this day will haunt me forever. Their little legs were all red from the bites. I just wanted to take them back home where it was familiar territory.

Calamine lotion, food, teddy and a good night's sleep, was just what the doctor ordered. We all felt better in the morning. Exhaustion had grabbed hold of us all quite hard.

My husband actually had a job lined up. I was impressed. He was starting for a tree trimming service that following week. He wanted warm weather; he was going to be outside in it.

So we set out to find a place to live. Not too far from his family we found a nice apartment complex. Townhouses, two bedrooms, 1.5 baths, dishwasher, two floors, laundry facility and a pool. I couldn't believe how nice it was and the price was pretty good too. We moved right in. We went down the road and purchased some beds and a couch. The apartment was pretty empty, but we finally had our own place to lay our heads.

By that night the hurricane was fast approaching. We were instructed by family to run down to the Piggly Wiggly and get canned food, bottled water, batteries, etc. It was total chaos. I had never seen such a thing! The shelves were bare, the place was a mob. After a few minutes prior feeling better about the move, my hopes were soon crushed with the doom of a hurricane.

We set up camp in a small closet under the stairs in our new apartment. We made it out to be an adventure for the boy's sake. We camped all night. We got lucky. It lost speed and momentum coming inland. The next morning we awoke to see what the storm had done. There was a lot of damage. Huge puddles of water, tree branches everywhere, screens from windows scattered about, along with trash and debris. I remember thinking, well that wasn't so bad. We cleaned up around our vehicles, our back yard and front steps. We went to Wal-Mart to continue shopping and set up house. Dishes, towels, anything and everything that we needed for day to day life. We had to replace pretty much everything, with exception on a few items that folks back home had given to us. We all needed summer clothes, the warm weather was not disappointing us. We could really enjoy this part of the change. I was starting to feel better. I had lost some weight in the past few months and it was good to buy some new clothes. I didn't recall the last time I had bought new clothes, I think it could have been school shopping, which had been years prior. When the boys were in need, they got new items, I always went without or just got pushed to the back burner. Just as many mothers do.

The week went well. We found our way around; we got settled in and comfortable. We went to the beach and discovered it was our favorite place. We could take a picnic lunch, pay five dollars to park for the day and enjoy the sun & sand. We were adapting to the heat and quickly acquiring very nice tans. We all enjoyed the sun. The boys were suffering with their hair and begged for it to be cut. So we all went, we all were going to get "trimmed up". Well, I was always told that I was not allowed to have a short hair style, by my husband. He was adamant that I was to have very "girly" hair and keep it that way. When it was my turn to sit in the chair, the stylist asked, "what would you like done?" I looked in the mirror and glanced at my husband. Finally, with great confidence I said, "CHOP IT OFF!!" Well to a hair stylist, that is music to their ears! She was excited and grinning from ear to ear. Which made me feel good, it made me smile too. I glanced back at the reflection of my husband and I thought by the look in his eyes he would have hurt me, given the chance. That look pierced my skin. I was a bit scared to leave the salon. She chopped it off all right. I loved it! She styled it and made comments that it was a very chic cut for me. The reactions I received from other patrons, were very complementary. Comments made were, that I looked younger, I looked glamorous, ooh's and ahh's...the reactions seemed to soften his attitude about my short hair cut. So from that point on, it was all about me being "cooler" with the mercury as high as it was.

He started his job. He seemed to like it. The boys started school a few weeks later. So I started looking for a job myself. I was discouraged there wasn't much that I was finding. One day I opened the newspaper and saw "bakery assistant wanted". Over the years I had dabbled in cake decorating and I really enjoyed it. So I called on the ad.

I liked her right off the bat, she was friendly. She asked if I would come down and meet with her. She gave me the directions and as I was writing them down, I started to get scared. Charleston? I have to go where? I hadn't driven that far by myself and I still knew no one. But I wanted this job! It sounded fun and it might be exciting. I was totally up for some fun in my life. I set out and drove the directions. Well that familiar I-26 turned into a nightmare, four lanes of traffic. It wasn't rush hour, but it wasn't quite my cup of tea either. My determination is what got me there. I wasn't turning back. I wanted the job AND I was scared that I would get lost. So I continued on. I turned a big sweeping corner in the highway and saw the biggest bridge I had ever seen. Panic settled in my stomach, like it was ole familiar territory. I was terrified of bridges, water & heights; all three of those things were right in front of me. Then, as if a little rainbow popped out of the sky, I saw my exit. It was before the bridge, oh boy, was I relieved.

I was now in Charleston, SC. Famous Charleston! I was where Rhett Butler went in Gone with the Wind. I was so excited, I was so proud of myself. I had driven there all by myself. That was a huge feat I established there that day.

I found the small bakery, had my interview and I was hired on the spot! It was a family owned business. Her husband was a chef and started the business catering out of this little whole in the wall that they now called a bakery. They were so busy that they needed to expand; it was all going to be based on James Island. The shop in Charleston was being closed and moving over with the rest of the business. That was why I was needed so badly. I felt incredible. I couldn't wait to tell my husband, I couldn't wait to start; I was so excited that I had found a job. I was no longer going to be a cashier. I felt as if I was moving up, and I had accomplished it all by myself.

My excitement soon turned to worry. The commute when I had to be there was horrible. I had never in my life seen traffic like that. Four lanes of traffic, coming to a complete stop, tractor trailers locking up their brakes and smoke rolling off the tires. I was late my very first day. The baker was there and didn't seem impressed. I couldn't blame him, what an impression was I making? I started a conversation with what exit I lived at and said "this isn't like back home..." he asked where I was from and I told him. His whole demeanor changed, he was from New Hampshire. He understood, he opened up and talked my ear off. He explained a lot of things about the area to me. We fast became friends. He and his wife didn't have kids yet...but we related to each other rather well. It was cool because I felt connected to New England, feeling as if I knew someone there from back home.

The days rolled on, things were becoming routine. I was enjoying my new life. I was making more money than ever, seven dollars an hour was way better than five back in Vermont. I talked my husband into trading in the car for something with air conditioning, the commute I had was brutal some days in that heat. We found a nice family car, four door, a/c, power windows. It ended up being a bigger payment, but I was happy with it. The months rolled by and we were doing well. On the weekends, we would get out and explore the state that we now called home. We visited different attractions in the area, there was not a lot of money but we liked living our new life there.

We had found a church and that was fast becoming our family, we had support there. We made friends with good people. We went to all the activities the church offered. I thought my marriage was as wonderful as the "Cleaver's". I was thinking that we had never been stronger and that maybe the move to the south was indeed a change that we had needed. I saw a part of my husband that I didn't know was there. We talked, we spent time together, as a family and as a couple. We were living a life that was good. We certainly weren't rich, but we felt and lived rich in love and family values. I was finally in a happy place. We had begun to heal from the tragedy we left behind.

At one of the church functions, there was a prophet they had as a guest speaker. He was an older man, very jolly and wise. I clung to every word that he said and preached. There came a time when he was done his speech, he was drawn to certain people sitting there in the audience. He would go to a person and look them in the eyes and tell them something that was very personal. Something that only God himself would know. Each person he approached was being spoken to directly from the Lord himself. The room was so warm and you could feel the presence of a higher power. I had always believed in God, but that night I felt him. This prophet looked around the room, searching faces and moving about as if directed to a particular individual, and he was. He turned and looked me straight in the eye. I began to shiver, as he came to me and hugged me. He told me things that I were true, he saw that I had struggled my whole life. He saw the hurt and he told me that I was loved. He said that he knew I was going to get through what I was going through and that he would walk with me. I stood there and cried. I was overwhelmed, hearing the words that he told me. He told me to trust in Him and not to lose my faith. Get down on bended knee and pray, to sit and read his word...Standing next to me was my husband. I glanced up at him and he was crying just as hard as I was. That prophet opened his eyes, as well as mine. He had known that I was in pain, but he didn't realize the extent of it. Someone that had never met me before was revealing things about me, that he didn't know. Someone was validating what I had tried to tell him. After that night, he started treating me differently, in a good way. Almost as if he understood more about me.

One weekend we discovered that our vehicles had been broken into. I was so upset, I felt violated and scared. The neighborhood that we found a new home in, wasn't so wonderful after all. We weren't as at ease as we previously had been. Friends from church told us about a mobile home park that was just families and safe. So we went to check it out and decided we wanted a mobile home. We found a used one and it was the most beautiful thing I'd ever seen. Garden tub, big kitchen, huge sunk-in living room, three bed rooms, the color scheme was hunter green & mauve. The best part was, we could afford it.

So the next adventure began. We were once again home owners. We were happy. Finally, I thought, we had the cat by the ass, so to speak.

Throughout the years my husband had job – jumped. Never staying anywhere for very long. South Carolina was no different. He finally found something he loved to do. He worked in a junk yard. I admit, he came home happy and relaxed. I continued at the catering company and I was doing a little bit of everything. I delivered bakery goods to the coffee shops around Charleston, in a van no less. I went places I never dreamed I could, the traffic was fast becoming, the way of life. I drove that van over that big, huge bridge all the time. Not even thinking twice about it. I was going to catering functions and waiting on the rich southern bells of the south. Beautiful women with southern drawls and that hospitality that was always referred to in the movies. I even catered at some of the confederate homes in Charleston, near the world famous Rainbow Row. I helped put together 300 boxed lunches for a movie crew that was filming on one of the nearby islands.

We went home for the holidays. We saw everyone that we missed and realized we were really homesick. We went back to South Carolina with heavy hearts. Going back to our new found life. Returning to work, for me to discover it slowed down so much, that my hours would only be a few a day. It certainly wasn't going to be enough to pay the bills. So my job search started again.

I found an opening closer to home at a cleaning company. I liked it. Working there I was able to go into homes you only dream of seeing the inside of, and I was cleaning them. Beach homes, beautiful homes, huge homes. They were homes you would see on the Life Styles of the Rich and Famous. I wasn't making as much money as I had been and I was starting to feel it in the bank account.

My husband had a brilliant idea of selling the truck to buy an older car, or hot rod potential he would say. It was a 1972 Dodge Charger. It was indeed pretty cool. They didn't make cars like that anymore and it was a work of art in my eyes too. But it needed a lot of work. He was content with it, but it depleted any money we had left from our house insurance from the fire. But it made him happy, so I didn't fight it.

A month or so moved on and the cleaning job was coming to an end as well. I wasn't making enough to pay the after school daycare. So we agreed I might as well get done and find something part time while the kids were in school. I had no luck. Our money wasn't stretching far enough. What food we did have, it was for the kids. I would go without, many nights.

The pastor of our church approached me one Sunday and asked for my help. So I went with him to a back room at the church. There were shelves and shelves of food. He said, "I want you to take enough for your family for a week." I was so embarrassed, but thankful. Then he asked me to bag up another week's worth of food and deliver it to another family that had no vehicle. Of course I would do that. That was so very rewarding. A house full of kids, a single mom trying to finish up college and the kids were starving. They were excited just to see a loaf of bread, the sad part was, I could relate. I managed to stretch our food for a few weeks.

Depression & fear started to set in. I was fast losing my courage and scared wondering what would become of us. I wasn't the only one feeling it. My husband suffered in silence. Until one Saturday night he had been over to his family's, or so I thought. He called me in a panic, "I don't know where I am..." he was crying. He was having what I know now, as a panic attack. I was there all alone, I had no idea what was going on. He finally calmed down enough to figure out where he was. It was the beginning of the end, of what we had started to build after devastation. What in just a few months time, we had accomplished, was falling apart as quick as it came to us. He started laying blame on me, and it was the start of the old monster inside, growing and smoldering once again.

The electric was shut off. The phone was shut off. I was fast losing my grip & faith. It was difficult to remember the words of that prophet that I met that night in that church that I loved so much.

We thought long and hard, we agonized for weeks about what to do. Someone from church paid our electric, we had no idea who. But we were grateful; it bought us a little time. My husband was coming home earlier and earlier from work. He was bringing in less and less money every week.

We swallowed our pride and contacted "home" for money. We took the plunge to file bankruptcy. At that point in my life, I thought that was the most difficult thing to face. I'd rather of gone through child birth again. I felt so ashamed of myself. I had fought the odds all of my life and I was allowing this situation to get to me. But there does come a point, where you have no choice and very few options.

We lost everything, for the second time in less than a year. We had no home, one less car and no confidence. We packed up and went home, having failed miserably.

Heading back north to familiar territory, I had a lot of time to think. I thought about the crazy turn of events over the past year. The ups & downs. Failures & accomplishments. Failure taking precedence in the front of my mind. The hurt I had in my heart. The tragedy we all had been faced with. The courage we had, just to go on. And the strength that was no longer there. Ten months in SC, what it did to me, good and bad. The feeling of homesick and the feeling of maybe belonging. Wondering if we should have just taken a long vacation to some where warm... All wrapped up into a bale of emotions that my heart & soul wasn't prepared for. Thinking that if this is what life is supposed to be like...I don't want any part of it. That feeling stayed with me for months.

That spring I was turning thirty and I was very depressed. I hadn't accomplished much, in my mind. And the marriage that I thought would survive anything just a few months before was just a hollow shell. It was a show. A very bad show. The man I was married to transformed into a monster. A ball full of nothing but anger. Lashing out at anything and everyone in his path. Life with his parents was cramped and suffocating. His grandmother offered us a few rooms. She needed help to keep her big house going and she'd love the company. We sold the Charger for money to pay rent for a few months. So we moved in. We had a room for our television and she had a couch. The boys had a bedroom and we had a bedroom. My husband found a job about 45 minutes away and bought a truck. Things were looking up a bit for us. But he was still very angry. I was on the hunt for a job too. I ended up at the department of employment and training office to see if they could help place me somewhere. There was nothing. They offered me a spot in a program with the state. I was eligible to take some classes at the college, two a semester. They would also place me in an office job for minimum wage for twenty hours a week. I was excited and hopeful. Finally things would start coming together. It was going well. I was back to no vehicle and places to be. I walked and took the bus. Classes were two days a week and work was just down the street from where we were living. Daycare was a mile or so away. So again – I was walking a lot. I persisted though, I kept going. I did homework after getting the boys home between 5-6pm. And when I didn't have dinner started, my evening was a struggle! There was an angry bear coming home from working & fighting traffic (which was nothing in comparison to SC) but I was expected once again to be Wonder Woman. My shield was wearing down and his grandmother saw every struggle I went through.

I completed one semester and I was half way through the program. I had set aside enough money to buy a cheap car. We went on the hunt. I found a little hatchback but they wanted $800, I only had $600. I told him that I would give him $600 in cash and he sold it to me! I was so proud of myself. I did the wheelin' n dealin' all by myself.

A few months went by and things were a little easier on me. He was still full of anger and I didn't know why or what to do about it.

He came home from work one night and declared that we were moving back to South Carolina. I couldn't even believe my ears. I was crushed. My boys were crying. He was all puffed up and full of himself. Telling me I had to quit my classes, quit my job and pack us up. I was so embarrassed.

After I quit the program and packed us up, living out of boxes, yet again. We got our tax refund and he decided that we would stay in Vermont and get an apartment. Again, I was in shock, I couldn't believe my ears. What were we going to do? How could he keep doing this to us?

Meanwhile, I'd quit the program, that I was so close to completing and he had quit his job. So per his demands we found an apartment and I was on a job hunt. He finally found a job in the town we lived in which I was hoping would be a good thing. No more commute, less stress and maybe he'd be easier to live with.

I applied everywhere, having very little office experience. I was trying to "sell" myself, so someone would give me a chance to prove myself. Finally I got a break, an office position. I wasn't keen on the company, but the one that hired me liked me and wanted to be that person that helped me get into a good job. For that I was thankful and it gave me a boost. It wasn't glamorous, it wasn't rocket science, but I became good at it. I started running parts of the office that weren't really required and I really stepped it up to prove myself. I was there for three years and I received raises frequently. I was feeling great about my career. No more cashiering for me.

Meanwhile my husband had still been difficult to live with. Same demands, job jumping, never staying places too long. I was working 50-60 hours a week, raking in the "big bucks", or so it felt. After a spell we decided that we needed a better car. So we found a dealer that worked with people that have gone through bankruptcy. I had my first car that only had one prior owner and it had less than 30,000 miles. I was scared because of the payment and what happened the last time we had a car payment. I would go through times of utter panic, which made me difficult at times.

As time went on, I got be friends with one of the guys I worked with. He was a nice looking guy, and treated me very well. Being at work so much I spent time with this guy. On the phone with him a lot and when I was left in the office alone, he was able to help me with questions I had so I wasn't making mistakes dispatching people where they shouldn't be. I started having feelings for him. One thing lead to another and I had a very short affair. I rationalized the whole thing because of my husband cheating on me, years prior. I never dealt with it, just swept it under the "rug". The rage and jealousy in my husband became too scary to bear. At that point he knew nothing; he was just a very possessive person.

So I asked my brother if I could stay with him. It was becoming more and more of a safety issue. That was a very difficult decision. I left the boys there because they were in school and I needed to figure out what I was going to do. I had the boys almost every weekend and when I brought them back to the apartment, it was a horror show every time. My purse would be hidden on me, so I couldn't leave. I'd get twenty questions, wanting to know what I had been doing and with who.

While I was living with my brother and the weekends that I had the kids, my husband was getting friendly with one of his friends from school. He hung out with the couple in school and they were going through separation as well. They were always doing things together and the boys didn't really like her. But he did, he always had and now she was paying attention to him. They were "in the same boat" so to speak.

I was gone for about two months. And my husband started to change, so I thought. I was really starting to think that perhaps it could work. So I went back. I wasn't honest with him about having an affair. I was terrified to tell him and I figured what did it hurt? I was able to move on from what he had done to me...

After I moved back into the apartment, that couple was getting back together as well. We thought that was pretty cool, so we planned a night out, dinner and dancing. The whole time at dinner my husband was talking about how beautiful "she" was. How wonderful "she" was. He went on and on. It was horrible. It was degrading. I wanted to crawl under the table. Her husband tried moving the conversation over to me. Saying that I looked very nice, asking me about work, anything he could to divert his so-called buddy's conversation about his wife. But he persisted in talking about HER. It really made me wonder why I moved back. He obviously didn't love me. He only wanted "control" and a house keeper, I felt anyways. So belittled and sorry for going back to him, I remember wishing that I was Samantha on Bewitched, so I could twitch my nose and have it over with. Where the hell did this guy come off doing this? Did I really deserve it? Was I really that bad of a person?

In the first month I was back, I regretted every single minute of going back to him. He was OK at first, nice and caring. All of a sudden I get a call at work from him. He tricked me into telling him that there was a guy I had been with. He was so angry. He told me that I had better get home at that moment or he would be at my work. So I left. I was almost to the apartment, I glanced in my rear view, and all I could see was a truck grill. That's it. It was right on the tail of my car. In an instant I glanced at the road and before I glanced back in the mirror again, I was rammed in my back bumper. This was a big lifted black truck, which happened to be driven by my husband. He'd bought it while I was moved out. He was a total and utter crazy man!! I caught a glimpse of his face in my mirror and I was terrified. The look in his eyes was of such hatred.

I arrived at the apartment and I tried to relax a minute to catch my breath. He stormed in the door, I regretted in that instant not driving directly to the police department. I was bombarded with a fist. Several times, getting my head bounced off the wall. Wishing that I would pass out... Things calmed down and I lay on the bed till I fell asleep. I awoke after dark; all I heard was the television. Next thing I know my head was being punched into the wall again. He was beating me repeatedly. He hurt my hand so bad I thought it was broken. Just as my head was getting ready to meet the wall again, my oldest son intervened and stopped it. That was the longest night of my life. I had to call out sick at work for a few days, my fingers where pretty bruised along with the rest of my body, but my hands couldn't be hidden.

I was then forced into quitting my job. I wasn't allowed to do anything by myself. Simple grocery shopping was a big deal. Going to the Laundromat, was a big production. I was reminded every day what a low life piece of pond scum I was.

I found a job, making more money than ever. It was a really good job. I knew I was really going to like it. I had to go away for training and I wasn't allowed to go by myself. My husband had quit his job and packed the kids up and we all went. I was so incredibly embarrassed!

I was working for a trucking company that was expanding to the area, so I was going to be around all kinds of guys. That aspect was not a good thing. The rage and jealousy was almost deadly some days. But I persisted in my career. It was the only form of escape I had. I worked every day, diligently. Still being constantly reminded what a horrible person I was. Apparently he had forgotten his affair. In his eyes, that was different.

Time went on and he was still job jumping, nothing ever stable. I never knew from day to day if I'd be the only one working. Every day was becoming a battle. Struggling with life, not seeing my family only once in awhile, and being made to feel that I had ruined someone else's life and that I didn't care a bit about my kids. My self esteem was zilch, zero, zip, NONE! I felt so low. I felt sad all the time. I couldn't laugh. It was all a struggle.

Then after my husband had actually been at a job for awhile, I started thinking this "slump" was over. Days were getting better. The reminders weren't so much in my face. The fits of rage were farther apart.

I was getting sick of apartment living. My father and I talked about it and he suggested looking for a house. He was planning on cashing in a life insurance policy to be split between my brother and I. So I now had a down payment. We looked and looked for months, searching for just the right spot. We finally found a cute little house. It wasn't perfect by any shot, but it had potential, I saw more there than what was. I thought maybe it was a new beginning and things would get better. It was something for us to focus on together.

We set out to painting the whole inside. Because of all the apartments we had lived in, I was really tired of white walls. I needed some color in my life, something fresh, and something that I could have control over and not have to ask the landlord for permission. I was the landlord now. I picked out different colors for every room. I let the boys pick their own colors. We had full weekends of paint and Spackle.

Along with being home owners, came other bills and projects. We put on new siding, got new appliances, remodeled the bathroom, and fixed the driveway. My brother did the work on the driveway, he was amazing. Just a few hours of work and it was transformed! My father was quite the woodworker, so he offered to make me some shutters. It made the house look more like a cottage, a home, a dream come true. I found a blue paint that was so pretty and I just fell in love with. I painted them, I was so tickled with the color I did the trim and the doors the same color. Then I started gardening, landscaping. It was becoming my escape. I fell in love with being outside at the crack of dawn, mulching and weeding. Seeing things that I put in the ground grow and flourish. How rewarding was that? Extremely! I had a focus and a hobby that got me outside and it was an interest that I shared with my father and step mother. So I saw them more often, they would stop by with plants for me and give me suggestions. I was growing more of a bond with the first man in my life, my dad.

Off and on through the years we had had several dogs. One reason or another they never stayed with us very long. Never being in a place that allowed it, except South Carolina and his grandmother's. It was a difficult thing to go through, growing attached to an animal and having it taken away from us quickly. So having our own place, with no landlord making those rules, the boys talked me into finding some kittens. What a simple joy I gave them in giving into their pleas, they each had their own. A short time later, against my will, we got a wolf/mix puppy. He was the cutest, cuddliest thing I'd ever seen. I vowed not to be the only one to take care of him and I secretly vowed not to become attached to him. But I failed miserably and ended up falling in love, he latched onto me because I took care of him. He would snuggle up next to me in bed. He was loyal, he gave me unconditional love and certainly bought me joy. A true, man's or in this case, woman's best friend, what better love than from an animal?

Well my husband wasn't cool with that. Over the years he had become very jealous. He was even jealous of the boys. And having this dog, it was like having another kid. I needed to tend to him, and it diverted my attention. He didn't like that, he didn't like me paying attention to something else. He wanted my focus to be on him. So he started beating the dog over stupid things he did. I believe he even made things up. It was breaking my heart. Every animal I had ever loved, he took away from me.

One day I get a call at work, my husband screaming at me because "my" dog had got into something and he hated him. He told me that I'd better get home to say good bye to the dog. I was so heart broken, I bawled the whole way home. When I got there the dog was all ready gone. I couldn't win. I was devastated. I'd lost my best friend, the only friend that I felt I had. He found any jealousy he could and held it with such force. A little part of my heart died right there in that moment and I was scared to love another, I couldn't even speculate having another animal...

I muddled through, day to day. Being sad and unhappy. I got through because I had to, for my kids. I started my days with the coffee. I had to make him his coffee and get him up and going for work. Make his lunch and get myself ready for work. Once he was out the door, I could sigh a little bit. Then I had to get the boys up and rolling, which was no easy task. By this time they were teenagers, they really liked to sleep and didn't like getting out of bed, especially to go to school. I had become a mother, a wife, a housekeeper, and I worked a job forty hours a week. There were days, I have no idea where my energy came from.

I always had to think ahead at 5 am. Get something out of the freezer for dinner. When I forgot, I paid for it dearly. Because when my husband got home from work, he got to relax on the couch with the remote in hand, and his woman had to make him supper. Yes, he was that barbaric. There were days I got home from work and crawled into bed and just cried. It felt like I was so alone. There were days that I just couldn't think of going on. It really pained me. I couldn't figure out for the life of me, what did I do to deserve this treatment? The head games, the control, the punishment that came if it didn't go exactly the way he wanted it to. We all paid consequences for things that were beyond our control.

One evening I remember how I paid for not having dinner done on time. He was in a rage, and calling me every word in the book. He wasn't getting his satisfaction of dinner in hand. He kicked over the coffee table and broke everything that was on it. One item being a big snow globe that I had treasured. It was a very expensive globe, it was beautiful. It was a holiday one, but I kept it out year round. It held a tea light candle on top, it had a button you push and the snow would move. Around the outside when you wound it up there was a Santa and his sleigh that went around. I didn't have a lot growing up, no extravagant items. So this snow globe was something very special to me. Well it was on the coffee table and it was in pieces everywhere. I couldn't believe what he had done. I cried so hard at the sight of that living room. My heart had been trampled on, once again. After his fit of rage was over, I was expected to clean up the mess that he had made...

I talked to my family once in awhile. I was starving for friendship. But I had no one. I'd talk to the boys, but they weren't into hanging out with me so much any more. They had their friends, they were teens and just not so much into being around me like they were years earlier.

My husband would get into these raging fits on the weekends. Whining that we had no money to do anything. When in reality we made the choice to have a nice home. So there were sacrifices. He quickly forgot about that. He would get so ugly, my insides were constantly on edge and I was in such turmoil. And the shards of glass that I tip toed over, were getting plentiful. I'd find any escape, laundry; cleaning; baking; gardening...

The topic of one weekends complaint came about vehicles. It was thrown in my face that I had had the nicer car, always. He never remembered the days I walked everywhere. It was all about what he had to supposedly sacrifice. So I gave in to the fight, we went down to the local Chevy dealer and talked to one of the sales guys. We test drove a couple cars and we decided on a nice Oldsmobile. It was similar to the car that we bought when we were in South Carolina. That tweaked a little fear in me. But we took the plunge and signed the papers. We actually ended up with twin cars, just different colors. He had wanted a maroon one so that was the one that he drove, at first. The second one was silver. I loved a silver vehicle, and I told him that I'd really liked the silver one. Well all of a sudden, he started taking the silver one. It was just another little nudge, saying "I'm boss, and you don't count" and "your voice won't be heard here"...

Another weekend not too long after the cars, he comes home with a Harley! No communicating, no nothing. He was happy and that was all that counted to him! It was a temporary fix for him. So he had a toy. He got me to go with him often. I admit, except for the speed where I was uncomfortable, I did enjoy it. We put on a lot of miles. We struggled with the house payment; two car payments and now the Harley.

We stopped at the Harley dealer one weekend for some event going on. They had just brought out a few models of that next year's bikes. One stuck out at me, just beckoning me over. It was the most beautiful bike I'd ever seen. Cobalt blue and it was all comfort, Harley style. The sales guy caught my eye and came over to talk to me. I was mesmerized by its beauty. I wanted that bike so bad. My husband came over to listen in on the conversation, jealousy motivating him over. I asked the salesman to crunch some numbers and it wasn't much more than the payment we had. I figured what the heck, you only live once and if I was forced into having a payment on a motorcycle, I want one that I had picked out, if possible. So we traded up. I wanted to get my license so bad so I could drive it myself. I was so happy with that purchase.

My husband was always getting friendly with other women. What he thought was being friends came across as, much more. He made many women think that they had a "chance" with him. Which I never understood. He thought he was a hot ticket with that Harley, and that he was a "great catch". Forgetting about me and the ring that was on our fingers making us man and wife. There was a girl in particular that stands out in my mind. She was a friend from his, high school days. She happened to be the sister of the one that he hung around with when I lived at my brother's. She was a single mom with a very cute little boy, he was in 1st or 2nd grade. He ran into her at a store while stopping to gas up the car and she was having car troubles. So he took it upon himself to help her, being the very helpful person that he was. (I say this with sarcasm...) He started stopping by her place on the way home from work and getting home later and later. So of course I was feeling more insecure, with a lot running through the back of my mind. Memories of his affair with my best friend, came flooding back to me. This friend of his from school was taking his time, which was a catch twenty two. As long as he wasn't home, he wasn't messing with me. I didn't have to jump at his barking orders. The holidays were coming and they didn't have much. I felt bad for them. I remembered being very poor and if it wasn't for help from others my kids would've gone without. So I agreed to help them for the holidays. I baked, shopped, the kids and I wrapped presents. And my husband delivered it all, taking all of the credit. It was wee morning hours when he got back. Nothing was said. Of course I didn't throw it at him like he did me, I was a bigger person than that. But, when I was five minutes late getting home from work. "Who is HE this time?" was the song and dance that I would get. I was on a very short leash and watched like a hawk. But it was fine and dandy that he was coming home that late.

One weekend he went over there and I had groceries to get. So I was occupied. Well I hurried so I wasn't questioned when I got home. He wasn't there. It had been at least two hours, so I scurried to put all the groceries away. I figured out dinner and did some house work. It got to be late in the afternoon and still no sign of him. The boys were at friend's houses and I was enjoying having the house quiet and to myself. But it made me wonder...after I had accomplished everything I wanted to. I sat down to relax and have a little control of the remote and watch some television. Thinking for sure that is when he would be coming home, I was never allowed to watch what I wanted on TV. If I started watching a program, he came in the house, he took the remote and watched what he wanted. So I gobbled up the time to myself, since the occasion was rare.

Meanwhile, the day light was fading fast. I tried to call his cell phone and there was no answer. I actually started getting worried. So I set out to check things out...see if he was at her place. His car was there. I just sat there for a few minutes trying to figure out what to do. Do I go to the door and knock? Do I just leave? What? So against everything in me, I approached the door, not sure of what I would find. I could see him sitting on the couch with her son watching TV. At first glimpse I thought it was nice, very cute. He didn't have a dad, and he was probably starved for attention from a male figure. Then I saw her walking, brushed by him, touching his leg and sitting next to my husband on the couch. It took my breath away. I was paralyzed standing there. Something made them look at the window and they saw me. I ran for the car. I had every intention of knocking, until I saw her. And I froze...so many things raced through me. I couldn't go through this again, he had done it once to me. I started having a hard time breathing and I felt really sick. I was pulling out of the driveway and he caught up to me, thoughts of running him over were right there, but I didn't. The first thing that he says is "it's not what it looks like..." and I said, "what does it look like?" If that statement didn't reek of guilt, I don't know what would. I started shaking and I didn't feel well at all. I was hell bent on getting away from him. The closer he got to me the faster my heart raced and I started hyperventilating. He says, "what's wrong with you?" I told him I had to go, I had to get to the hospital.

I was having a panic attack. Anxiety and depression is what I was diagnosed with. They prescribed medication for me. I continued to have my sad times and still came home from work to crawl into bed. I would spend a lot of time with the blinds closed and the covers over my head. It was a "safe" place for me. Just like an innocent child that was afraid of the boogie-man, thinking that the covers were there to protect them. My husband would be so mad that I was in bed. He made me go see my doctor, sure that there was more wrong with me. I knew what was wrong with me, it was him. But I reluctantly went back to my doctor. Every six months or so, adjusting my medication, just to keep me on an even keel.

At night I would fall asleep on the couch watching TV. Sleep was and had become an escape for me. The solace I found in shutting my eyes, was the only comfort I felt. He thought that if I was able to be awake and cheat on him years prior, I guess I should be good enough to keep him company and stay awake for him. He was constantly throwing things of that nature at me. He would often make me do things that I was not comfortable with. His plea was that if I could give myself up to another man I would have to show that I love him more than anything and do anything that he asked of me. Including the unthinkable in the bedroom. I was humiliated quite often. No matter what he asked and how far I had allowed it to go, (of course, not having much choice) it was never good enough. He pushed and pushed, harder every time. As soon as it was over, it was forgot, that quickly. There was no way to pacify him. Nothing I did mattered or was ever appreciated.

I wasn't allowed out much, but I was friends with my brother in law's girlfriends over the years. They were the only ones that my husband let me out of the house to go visit on occasions. I went over to their house one night and she wasn't home. But her daughter was. She had been grounded and was not to have any friends over. When I got there, she was there with a friend from school. I questioned her on it and she begged me to take her home so she wouldn't get in trouble. It was getting late and very dark. I finally gave into her. I tried to call the house to let my husband know that I was doing something for our niece. There was no answer, I left a message. I told her that the deal would be, she would continue trying to call my house and let him know that I was taking her friend home. Of course, she agreed.

I asked the girl where she lived and she said on the other side of town. Little did I know, this girl was in a different school district. She would tell me where to turn when we approached a road. I was starting to get nervous. She was taking me way out of town. And I ended up about fifteen miles away. She thanked me repeatedly. I knew she was home safe and to me at that moment I was satisfied. By this time it was well into the evening, it was about 9:00. I sped home. When I arrived my husband flew out the door with rage in his eyes. "where have you been?...who were you with?!" I was greeted with a few slaps on the face. I tried to explain, but he wasn't listening. I went right to the phone to call my brother in law's house so our niece could tell him the story. Well by that time her mom was home and of course she couldn't be caught in a lie. So I paid for her lying. She denied that I had been there, she denied that I had given her friend a ride home. I paid in ways that that girl would never dream. I was accused of cheating on my husband, I didn't sleep much that night. And when he was tired in the morning from staying up, I was blamed for him not sleeping.

Later that summer we participated in a toy run on the motorcycle. It was a drive to benefit kids in the hospital. I had watched it on the sides of the road for many years, I got goose bumps when I saw the hundreds of bikes speed by me. Knowing what it stood for and all those "tough" bikers, doing for kids. I was finally going to be a part of it. I was so excited. Feeling and hearing the rumble all around you. Hundreds and hundreds of bikes coming together for a wonderful cause. It was so incredible. It was a beautiful day, not just with the sun shining on us, but the sight of the toys all on the State House steps when the ride was all over.

We ended up going to a local bar that was doing a BBQ and having music for the bikers. I was having fun at first, we were going to only have a few drinks, eat and go home. Well my husband's drinks turned into a lot. I stopped having fun about three hours into this adventure. Which it was late afternoon by then. He was flirting with the bartender, saying things to her that a married man shouldn't be saying to another woman. I couldn't believe my ears. It certainly wasn't the first time he had shocked me with his words. I asked him repeatedly to take me home. I was done having fun. It was getting very late. The next thing I know, it's 11:30 or so. Pretty late for people that didn't go out very much. Getting him to finally leave was a struggle and he had to of course thank the bartender for her hospitality. I wanted to crawl under a rock. I was fantasying about a truck coming out from no where and hitting me. Just to put me out of my misery. I was scared getting on the bike with him and I had good reason. He terrified me. Racing at speeds he shouldn't of been.

Once the wheels were in our driveway I jumped off. Told him what a jerk he'd been driving like that. Oh boy, did I regret opening my mouth, I ended up regretting the whole day. We ended up fighting like no other fight ever. I got to a point where I just wanted to sleep and tried going in the house, he wouldn't allow it. He yelled at me on our front lawn, he shoved me down on the ground and kicked me. I was hoping that a neighbor would be up and hear the commotion, enough to call 911. The whole time I was on the ground, wondering, what on earth did I do to deserve this treatment. Was I really a bad person? I had tried so hard! I worked hard. I did everything for my kids. I was running out of steam. He had stripped me of my confidence. He told me I was worthless. He told me I was fat. After he had gained a hundred pounds since we'd got married. I was alienated from all my friends and torn away from my family. I didn't want to deal with the pain any more. The last time he kicked me to the ground, I found a sharp rock and tried digging it into my wrist. Of course it didn't work. He saw what I was doing and said there was no way I was leaving him, especially that way...I managed to get in the house and grab the keys to the truck we had bought for the boys to learn to drive. I ran out to try and get in it, he was right behind me. He slammed my arm in the door. The pain I felt was so bad, I was wishing that the rock I had just had, minutes before, had done the job. So I could die. I cried and cried. I thought about running, but had no idea where to go. Awhile later I was in the house trying to get an ice pack. My arm was swelling up and I could feel nothing but the pain. Before I could get to the kitchen I was dragged to the front door and my head was banged against it a few times. Then I heard the screams. It wasn't just me screaming now. It was my guardian angel, once again saving me. My oldest son was watching TV, by this time he was a senior in high school. As tall as his dad and going into the army after graduation. He intervened once again. I was so grateful he was there.

Totally, utterly exhausted and in so much pain I couldn't bare it, I cried myself to sleep. I slept on the floor with my boys in their room that night. I felt a bit safer in their presence. When I awoke in the morning, I knew that part of me had died that previous night. I knew that was the last time he would lay a hand on me.

I suffered through Sunday and work on Monday. I drove myself to the hospital right after work. I couldn't take the pain any longer. I had to think up some lie as to how I hurt myself. One of the first questions the nurse asked was, "is there any domestic violence at home?" Without even looking at my face to see the terror in my eyes, not moving her head from the position of looking at her computer screen. She typed in my answer of NO. Why didn't she persist? Couldn't she feel the fear in me? So much for woman's intuition. My arm wasn't broken, but it was sprained real bad and they put it in a brace.

When I got home I went about my business making dinner. The boys questioned me about my arm and felt bad for me. They helped me as much as they could. Of course my husband didn't even bat an eye. His concern was the usual, dinner and clean clothes for the following day.

I took a lot of grief at work the next day. My story was pretty lame. Months later the ones that picked on me found out the truth. I secretly hoped that they felt like the scum I was made out to be by my husband.

My husband was a truck driver at that point and met one of my drivers on his route quite frequently. They would talk on the cb. My husband wasn't aware of the story I told at work. He opened his mouth and said "did she tell you what I did to her?" he left the fight part out, but he told the truth about the injury. Well that driver called me from his first stop. He asked me what was going on. I tried laughing it off but he saw right through it. I was so embarrassed and so grateful at the same time. A friendship began that day. I don't know if it was out of pity or what it was. But that was my next guardian angel.

I'd always liked this guy. Such a nice person. Laughed all the time. Always a pleasure to be around. When he shared a glimpse of my secret, I felt a connection to him. Although he was much older, I kind of started having a crush on him.

Between August and the end of October, just after my oldest son's eighteenth birthday, I found my "OUT".

I was so tired, so sick of the head games, the abuse mentally and what had happened the day of the toy run. I'd had it, I was just in Lew of my escape.

I was ordering pizza from work one Friday night for my husband and the boys and was going to a candle party that one of the driver's wife was having. But that morning I had forgot to leave a check for the pizza. So my husband was calling trying to track me down to run the checkbook home. When I got there I was bombarded with questions and called every name in the book. My skin started to crawl . Any joy I had in me had disappeared with the wind. The air in my sail was gone. And I knew in that instant it was the last night I'd be in that house of terror. More words were said and my youngest son got involved. But he wasn't on mom's team, he had joined the dark side. He was as big as his dad, both towered over me. My oldest son was at a friend's house for the night. Things got pretty heated up and I tried fighting back. The fight moved to the bedroom, which is where the guns were kept. My husband proceeded to get a gun and was digging for bullets. I grabbed the phone, dialed 911 and he tore the phone out of the wall. Meantime, my son saw red and had his hands around my neck. Yes - my son! He didn't want his dad going to jail. Thank God 911 calls back on a hang up. I ran to the kitchen to get the other phone and my husband beat me there. As if he had surrendered, he answered it, he talked to the dispatcher for a moment and said "it's for you..." handing me the phone. She dispatched two units to the house. She kept me on the phone until the police reached me. She also needed to be sure that the gun was not in a hand before the door was knocked on.

Meanwhile my husband was calling me all kinds of names. Both he and my son were screaming at me. The dispatcher tried her best to tell me not to listen and calm me down. Finally the officers showed up, they had the gun and took my husband and son outside. One of the officers stayed inside with me, talking to me and asking what I'd like to do. He was giving me some options and I decided to leave. I figured it would be easier for me to leave than it would be for them. So I packed a bag and the officer helped me out to my car. When I stepped out that door and into the night air, I saw a glimmer of hope in the sky. And then I got a real deep sinking feeling, the sight of my husband talking to the other officer there. They were joking and laughing, it was someone that he had gone to school with. That just did not settle right with me. I was given instructions on where to meet the battered woman rep and while that was happening, my brother and his wife pulled up. They had a feeling of needing to stop and see me...

They automatically followed me to the police station and when I got out of the car my brother's arms were tightly wrapped around me. Once again my baby brother was there for me, ready to take charge. I didn't even have to call him for his support and love, he just showed up. They were there with me in the police station while I filled out the report, giving me Kleenex and encouragement. I was offered battered woman's services but I was too scared to go because one of my husband's jobs was at the state food bank, and he knew where the shelters were! I wasn't willing to endanger others, so I declined. My brother spoke up and said he would be sure I was safe. When we were done there, he found a safe spot to park my car. He got me something to eat and took me to the ATM so that I wasn't left without money. Then he drove me to our mother's house. A safe haven for me. It was as good as it got for the time being. My brother and his wife stayed until they thought I was calm enough to sleep.

I laid in the room I'd grown up in that night. Breathing. Sighing. Battered. Bruised. Relieved. Happy and scared. But for once in a long time, I slept well.

Challenges I faced that week were difficult. Restraining order & court. Making sure the police took all of the guns out of that house. I was told that I needed to get a copy of the police report for court, so that the judge knew what had been reported. But to my dismay, there was no report filed. The police officers that came to my house that night that my life as I knew it had come to an end, did not file a report. On top of everything, I lost faith in the local law enforcement. Panic set in, I thought I was doomed. I thought my life was depending on that report to get this restraining order in place. I was running scared in my mind, thinking I would be forced to go back to that house. I was scared that he would stalk me and make my life even more of a hell if the court didn't rule this in my favor.

My mother went with me to the courthouse. We met up with the battered woman rep from that night. I sat in that big court room in front of three judges, with my husband across the room about twenty feet from me. I was terrified. The judges asked me questions and wanted to hear why I needed this order in place. Very emotionally I told my story. It was then my husband's turn. He told his side and the only words that I remember were, "...the gun wasn't for her..." One of the judges in particular was astonished by what he just heard. Later on my mother said that that judge's jaw dropped. I was granted the permanent restraining order. I felt a little safer. He couldn't be near me without there being consequences. I knew I was heading in the right direction.

I ended up getting close with that guy at work and I moved into his house. I thought I was falling in love with him. So there I was going through a divorce and trying to grasp hold of a stable life. I spent as much time with my boys as I could. My youngest and I had a long talk. It took a long time to gain trust between the two of us. He didn't remember what had happened that night. But we were all able to move on. I knew the boys were in need of more than I could give them. I did the best I could. They felt the effects too, it wasn't just about me. It never had been, I had stayed and endured as long as I did, for them. I hoped everyday that I didn't do more harm, than good. My whole life had been for them.

Just after I left my husband, left that abusive marriage. My brother and his wife went to Florida for the winter. My brother was laid off in the winters and would go to Florida for warmer weather, relax and maybe work part time. They talked me into going on a trip to see them. My brother had been going down there for years and had always wanted us to come down there. So here was my opportunity to do it. No husband telling me I wasn't going anywhere. I discovered that I had wings, I had freedom. Freedom to do what I chose. My wings had always been there, they were just broken and needed healing. So I ruffled my feathers. I took a trip to Florida. I flew all by myself. I figured out where I needed to go at the airports, all by myself. My wings started to open. I had never ever gone on a trip like that alone. It was a hat I felt very comfortable wearing. It wasn't my first time flying. I had gone to Disney World when I was a kid, with my dad and brother. So this was my second time flying. That aspect of it wasn't really scaring me. But just having been through the past 16 years under someone's thumb. I was just scared to be out on my own. It was just what I needed after the ordeal that I had survived. It was a really good trip. It gave me some confidence and independence. It brought me closer to my brother and his family. They had a little girl and she was my pride and joy. It was refreshing being there with them. We did a lot. We went to Universal, Silver Springs, Daytona Beach, we even climbed a lighthouse, one of the tallest in the United States. For three people that do not like heights, that was quite a feat. For me personally, I felt like I was on top of the world. Not just in the lighthouse, but I finally felt free. The memory of that climb will forever be with me. There I was, with my brother and he was leading the way. He would stop and encourage my sister in law and I. Again, my brother was there for me. It wasn't a huge struggle that I was going through at that moment, but yet it was. Just as he always has been, he was there to cheer me on.

Shortly after that trip they sold their house in Vermont and moved down to Florida full time. I think I had a bit of resentment. They were leaving me and they were taking away my niece, who meant a great deal to me. I kind of felt abandoned. But that angel would not forget me.

My oldest son graduated that following June. I was so proud. A few days later, my divorce was final. Later on that same day, my son was being picked up by his recruiter to go off to basic training at Fort Knox. So I went to the house and helped him pack. I spent a last afternoon with him. So here it was, both of my sons with me in their bedroom, in the house that I wanted so badly and loved so much. I'd given up so much to stay alive. I was crying, standing there with them. Looking at them both. A new beginning for all three of us. A chapter closing on a horribly painful life for all three of us.

Little did I know my ex husband had plans that day too. He yelled to the boys to come upstairs. I stayed in the basement, packing for my son. I wasn't so fearful by then. He had no hold on me. The boys were back downstairs in ten or fifteen minutes. They announced, "dad just got married..." Neither one of them was happy and I couldn't believe my ears. Even after we were divorced, he was still shocking me with his actions. SA la vie...

The recruiter arrived and waited on our tearful good byes. I knew I was saying good bye to my baby. I knew the next time I saw him, he would be a man. That was as difficult as the divorce, if not more painful. My story really began with him. My life really began when he arrived into my life. And here I was eighteen years later... My youngest son and I spent that afternoon together. Sad and scared for my son, his brother.

When I dropped him back to the house, his father dropped a bomb on me. He was taking my son and his new family to South Carolina. Talk about a day of shock. In a way I felt like I was grieving. This man that I had been married to for 16 years was ripping my heart out once again. I knew my son was happy to go to the warmth. But not to leave me. He suffered just as his father did in the winter with the cabin fever and feeling of being trapped in the Vermont snow. So I knew he would like that aspect.

So there I was - stuck - left dealing with selling the house and one car that he just abandoned to me. I was depressed and ready to throw my hands up. But I got through it, I managed to keep it together enough. I made one house payment by myself and it was sold! I walked away owing nothing and just a few thousand in my pocket. That was bittersweet. I held onto both cars and struggled through.

One weekend my new guy and I went out to dinner with another couple. It was very pleasant, it was very relaxing. I had never really had that with someone. Getting out and being able to actually enjoy an evening with friends. No arguing. No jealousy. No control what-so-ever. It was something that I liked very much. We were sitting there eating and a woman came up to our table. It was my ex husband's grandmother, the one that we lived with after coming home from SC. She came up to me and surprised me with what she said. She hugged me and told me that I would forever be her grand-daughter. I was so touched. She knew the struggles that I encountered. She understood, my leaving her grandson. She didn't particularly agree with much of what he did. And she told me that, right there in that restaurant. It made me feel very good inside. It made me feel as if, it wasn't in my head. I truly was the victim here and she was one person that saw it. I was very grateful for her coming up to me and telling me what she did.

Time went on, I bought my youngest son a cell phone, and added him on my plan so it was free to talk to him. I received news that my oldest son was graduating from basics. So I started planning a trip to Fort Knox. My ex husband was going to be there, I knew my son would be happy that we would be there to see him graduate. I made arrangements for my youngest to stay with me at the motel. It was going to be awesome. I was so excited to be seeing them both.

I smothered my youngest in lots of hugs n kisses. I spent every minute with him. We were able to go to the base the next day for family day, we were actually blessed with his presence all day. He was transformed. I couldn't believe my eyes. Who in the world was this person? No long hair. No "grudge" look going, clean shaved, perfect posture, no earrings and saying yes sir and yes mam. I was so proud that was my boy! That was MY boy! It had all begun with him. He was all grown up and ready to take on the world.

Graduation was so cool. To see hundreds of soldiers marching, little did I know he was going right onto the bus and right to the airport. We weren't going to see him again, I was shocked, we were so sad. We went back to the motel with heavy hearts.

About an hour later my cell phone rang. I heard the most wonderful voice on the other end. My son was calling from the airport. "MOM come see me..." of course we jumped in the car and headed to Louisville about an hour away. I'd never driven so fast. We didn't even stop to tell the boy's father. My son & I just went! It was our little secret, an afternoon with both boys before the oldest went off to be stationed in Oklahoma. That was a gift from above. That, to this day, I cherish.

That following morning saying good bye once again to my youngest, I was very emotional. Not knowing when I would see either one of my boys again. I over heard my ex husband saying that some of the parents went to the airport to see their kids after graduation. My son pipes up and says "that sucks, we could've seen my brother..." we looked at each other with a little smirk and a twinkle in our eye. We had a secret to bury deep in our hearts. That was the beginning of the healing between the boy that had his angered hands around my neck & I. That was an incredible long weekend, there in Kentucky. I had also grown up in that time. I'd found independence. I discovered there were things that I could do. I would've traveled the world to be with my two boys.

The fall after basics graduation, I found that not everything was a struggle, I had good in my life too. Despite missing my kids. I was blessed with a baby Shih Tzu. I don't think that when he was purchased, he was entirely meant to be my dog. But I was in love. I was scared to love him because of my history with animals. I became very attached to this little bundle of fur. He was the light of my life. My joy when I was down. A snuggler when I needed a hug. A doggie kiss and a tilt of his cute head when I was crying. I'd had no relationship with a dog as I did with him. After everything that I had been through he was my knight and shining armor. He greets me every night with his tail wags and happiness. He loves me so unconditionally. He is just what I have always needed.

The court had ordered me to pay my ex husband child support, which was a lot of money.

One hundred dollars a week. Yes it was unfair, I guess it was the price I paid for having the good job. The whole deal was unfair. He took the motorcycle and I was stuck with everything else.

I received a call one day from him saying that he was bringing my son back to Vermont. That was his "pitch". But he needed money for the rental truck. So I finally had the upper hand. It was me that he was bowing down to. I was his last resort. So taking control of the situation. I told him how it was going to work. I wanted the motorcycle and I wasn't going to pay him child support. If he was bringing me my son back, he would be with me. I wouldn't be giving him a red cent. He agreed. So I paid for the truck on my credit card, it was only $600, a small price to pay for my son being home with me.

A few days later my son was home. He called me to come pick him up at his grandparents. He told me that he had hurt his ankle. So when I got there I looked at it. It was bruised and swollen. Two days before he had fallen off the back of the rental truck when they were loading their stuff up. He drove his father's car 1200 miles with a broken ankle! He ended up having surgery, it was so bad! My hatred towards that sorry excuse for a man, my ex husband, was growing stronger and stronger by the day. But I had my son, and put him back in school, trying to give him some stability.

We went to Oklahoma that Thanksgiving to be as much of a family as we could. My boys and I - that was my family. It was a good trip. We spent the weekend at the motel, eating at different places & just relaxing. One of my son's buddies was alone on base for the holiday so we included him. One night they asked me to drop them down town for a few hours. The deal was they would call me when they were ready to be picked up. They ended up at a strip club and called me about 2 am for a ride. My son's buddy couldn't believe he was calling me. And when they got in the car he was telling me all about the club. That was how close my kids and I were.

I sat at a restaurant with them, watching them talk and laugh. I remember thinking how lucky we were. They were going to be OK. I was going to be OK. We were surviving after all the trauma. I was so proud of them and myself. We had really come a very long bumpy road, and still had all our parts and each other.

My son came home on leave a few months later. He was going to get a loan and buy his dad's car from me, actually, we re-wrote the loan with him as the primary. I was his co-signer. That was a big relief for me! One payment down, two more to go. On his leave, he dropped the bomb on us that he was marrying his high school sweetheart while home and take her back with him to Fort Hood where he was now stationed.

So we scurried about, to throw together a wedding and I had such a bad feeling about it all. They were married, drove back to Texas as husband & wife, so proudly in that car he just bought.

After I got rid of the house and one car payment. I decided I was going to buy a four wheel drive vehicle that I had always wanted. Something of my own. I set out looking at all kinds of things. H2's, Rav4, a small truck...and I test drove a Jeep. I found what I wanted. I didn't go extravagant, I went with the "middle model". It was four wheel drive, it was the color I wanted, silver, it had only 6 miles on it. It was brand new and I negotiated the deal all by myself. I got a payment that was less than the two cars payments I had been handling. I was so proud of myself. It was a little boost that my ego needed. I had a little confidence that was never there before.

Later that summer I sold the Harley. What a relief that was. I was slowly getting there. But I had a ton of credit card debt because of all the trips I took to be with my kids. I also went a little crazy buying clothes, because I had gone so many years with the restraints of nothing new for myself to wear. I had been told all through my marriage, that there was no need for me to have new clothes. So...when I sold the Harley, I made a little profit. Paid the loan off and one of my credit cards. I felt pretty good.

I was still in and out of depression, but the medication was working for the most part. I would go through highs and lows. When I was low, I was really low.

Leap year was coming and there was an ole wives tale or something that I had heard on the radio, that a woman could propose to a man on Feb 29th. I thought the man I was with was the one. He was good to me. Made sure I had good tires and oil changed in my Jeep. All that "guy" stuff. He didn't hold me back from doing anything. I went on trips, with my kids and my girlfriends. I finally had friends in my life. I wasn't on a leash, at all. I wasn't made to feel like I had to be a slave to the house and cook dinner at a certain time. It was what I thought was good.

So I planned a nice romantic dinner. I had gone through bags and bags of conversation hearts to find all of the ones that said "MARRY ME", and I put them into a little box with a ribbon on it. I popped the question. Which ended up being a major mistake. The biggest one that I had made in a really long time. I got a speech on "why do you need that?"..."you know I love you..." he was yelling it at me. My heart was broken, we were never to speak of that night again. I felt as if I had made an utter ass of myself. I set myself up for heartache. I opened my heart up to someone that I trusted so much. And in minutes, my hopes and dreams were destroyed.

I then went into a deeper depression, there was no coming out quick on this one. I would lay around on the weekends and cry. Dwelling on what a loser I felt like. Always being left alone in the house to occupy myself. He was always out in the garage, working. He would come in the house once in awhile and I would be asked what was wrong. I was never heard, so I stopped talking about my "troubles". I knew I was just wasting my life there. It wasn't going any where. I knew if I didn't swallow a bottle of pills, I would have to find change. My only salvation was my puppy dog. He would snuggle and lick my tears. Listen to me when I needed to air my frustration, tilting his head and looking up at me with those big brown eyes. I imagined him saying, "mommy, it's okay..."

I did have friends in my life. I had caught back up with a girl I went to school with and had always been close with. She was back in my life and it felt good to have someone to talk to. It took some time to work back up to what we had lost. But it was finally getting there. The friend that got my ex husband and I together was also back in my life. That was really wonderful too. For so many years, she thought that she had done something wrong. She had no idea what I was up against. We lost so many years and we had a lot of catching up to do. I was learning how to be a friend all over again, because I had forgot what it was like. In order to have friends, you have to be a friend. Every time we were together, I was learning something new.

I got word that my son was being deployed to Iraq. I was beside myself. I was so upset. It was a mother's worst nightmare come true. I was living & breathing it. He was bringing his wife back home while he was over seas. And in the meantime he and his brother had decided his brother would house sit in Texas while he was gone. Between him, his brother and their father, they decided the youngest would quit school, because he was struggling there any ways. So all these decisions had been made without my knowledge. So here we go again, I'm losing my boys to miles apart. They were confident in the whole thing and the boys had never been closer. When he came home to bring his wife, he showed up with a new vehicle. Funny thing was he got the same Jeep I had, only a little older. I thought that was pretty funny.

That good bye was very tearful, I again had no idea when I would see my boys next. We kept in close contact through the next month. When my son was being dropped off for his flight, the boys called me on speaker phone so we could say good bye and hear the voices that made us feel more secure. A lot of tears, anxiety was high for all three of us. It was a hard day. The unknown scaring me, not knowing when my son would be able to call me again, and the fact that my baby at 17 years old, was in a state all by himself so many miles from me. It was a battle. One going off to battle for his country. A battle for one to find himself and keep his brothers place occupied. And a battle of keeping myself from going insane, worrying about the two elements of my life that had always kept me going. The prospect of losing either one of them, made me sick.

My youngest son grew up quite fast down there by himself. He found out that his brother was behind on every single bill he had. So we had some work to do, getting that fixed. I was trying to keep the electric on so my son wasn't sweltering to death in the heat. And he was getting more and more behind bills in the mail everyday. That first month or so was quite a struggle. But I was very proud of him, he managed his brother's finances quite well. And got him back on track, actually got some bills eliminated altogether.

At the same time he was there house sitting in TX, his father and his new family moved to FL. Not very far from my brother. They had always been friends throughout the years. I saw it as my ex going there to "mooch" off my brother. I'm not sure how that all went. It wasn't really my concern. But I did hear tid - bits from my son once in awhile and it made me giggle. The one that inflicted pain on me, was still struggling in life, moving around like a gypsy, never staying at a job. Pretty pathetic actually. I got news that my ex husband had been put in jail. I was secretly doing a happy dance. I thought, finally, he would get his! His wife had gone and maxed out a credit card in his name. Right fully upset about it, just not going about showing his anger in an appropriate way. He was physical with her. She too was forced to go to the emergency room. Only this time, he was not as lucky as he was when he was married to me. He went down to the hospital to see what was taking her so long. He was met by the police. He was taken to jail for the harm he had done her. He used his one phone call to call his ex brother in law, my brother. I don't know if it took him that long to really see the true colors or what it was. But he didn't call him back, my ex husband spent the weekend in jail. Sometimes, life has a way of giving you a smile that no one can comprehend. That news was pure and utter happiness to me. Not for the harm he inflicted on another woman, but the fact that she had the courage to do what I did not.

A few months after my son had been in Iraq, my daughter in law announced that she was pregnant. I was going to be a Grammy! We were all excited. I was involved right through and I was there for the birth. My son was on the cell phone and heard his daughter's first cries. It was incredible. When she was born, it was about half way through his tour and he was able to come home to meet his baby girl. Having wanted a girl so badly myself, I was so excited. That baby wouldn't ever want or need for anything, not as long as I was around! My son was so happy, he was happy to be home and be with his wife. He was a dedicated husband and father. He had grown up even more than the last time I had seen him. He was all bulked up and more handsome than ever. It was a very fast two weeks and before we knew it, he was on a plane back over seas. It was a tearful good bye at the airport. A new daddy kissing his baby, a hug and holding on for dear life from his mother. People coming up to him, shaking his hand and saying thank you. I was so proud that that was my son. I was sad beyond words and proud of what he had done thus far in his life.

Time went by and I had taken the baby every weekend for a few months. My daughter in law had been deemed unstable, she was battling with post baby blues and depression. Between her mother and I, we were nurturing that baby. I was very attached to her. She had fast become the light of my life, she put a twinkle in my eye again. My dog wasn't jealous of her either, he was a little mother hen, when she cried, he was right there beside her.

I received a call from my son's mother in law one afternoon. I was nervous, thinking something was wrong with the baby. Some thing was wrong all right, she dropped a bomb on me. She told me that her daughter's ex boyfriend had ordered paternity tests. I questioned why. Why on earth would he? Why would he ever be involved with my grand baby? Apparently, right after my son's deployment, she was back in his arms. My heart sank. My poor son's heart was going to be broken. I had no way to get a hold of him, except through email. So I sent him a message to please call me as soon as he was able to, I didn't care what time it was. So it was a waiting game. To hear from him half way around the world and for a test that we all crossed our fingers, would be in my son's favor.

I got the call about a week later, one evening, relaxing on the couch, enjoying TV...in the gentlest of voices she told me that the little girl I cherished so much, was not my grand baby - my son was not a father. I was devastated. I loved her so much! It was a connection in my mind, with my son, who was on the other side of the world. Too far for me to wrap my arms around and comfort. That rug was ripped out from under me fast! I don't think I have ever cried so hard in my life. I had no idea what my son knew. But the following day I got that answer. He called me at work. What he was going through was a million times worse than the pain I was feeling. My baby was hurting and he was too far for my reach. He was losing his grip fast and I lost the phone connection. I got a hold of the Red Cross and because I didn't know what was going on, I told them that he may be suicidal. Within hours his Commanding Officer called me. He assured me that his rifle was taken from him and that he would be with him all that weekend. I felt a little better. He called me again with an update a few days later and said that my son would be calling me soon.

He called and he sounded light years away. I heard the little five year old boy that I used to know. He was hurting and I couldn't fix it. There was no kissing this boo-boo, no bandage that would cover the wound. He told me that he wanted to adopt her. He knew how special that was because he was in her shoes. I was so proud of him and I felt the same way. I wasn't ready to let that little blessing and joy go. That fantasy was short lived. The paternal father was getting custody of her. I was blessed with her one last weekend, my son knew I had her and he called to say good bye to her. Even though she was only months old, she heard him say I love you sweet baby. She was gone to us, as quickly as she came to us.

That Thanksgiving I flew to TX to be with my son. The thought of him being there all by himself was making me sick, it was just the mother in me. He and I had become so close. We had the best time. He had lost weight since he moved down there and he looked good. We did so many things, anything that he wanted to explore, we did. We went to restaurants that he wanted to try. We rented a PT Cruiser and drove down to San Antonio. We spent the day there, there was so much to do. We went to the Tower of the Americas, the Alamo, we walked the River Walk. It was such a beautiful city, such a warm and sunny day. I felt like a kid again. I felt so free. I felt better after my time there with him. It gave him some company and it broke up his routine. It was a really good visit.

My son announced that he was divorcing his wife and I was rather excited for him. She had put him through enough. It was a chapter to close and he was moving on. He finished out his tour and made it safely home. He was back on U.S. soil and I was so happy. The two boys drove home about two weeks later, for a reunion of all time. We were all so happy to see one another and hug. For the first time, I think they were just as starved for my hugs as I was for theirs. By that time their dad was out of jail and back in Vermont. So the boys were able to see him as well. No matter how much I despised the guy, that was the only decent thing about him. He was their father, good or bad, he adopted one and loved them both the same. I will never be grudge him that.

I was able to take a road trip back to Texas with my boys. That was a trip of a lifetime. I was the greatest gift ever. No girlfriends or any one else around taking their attention, just us three! I had the two most wonderful guys in my life with me. I was on top of the world. I drove most of the way which was pretty awesome in itself. When I got tired they would take turns driving. I learned things on that trip that I will never forget. We saw things together and made memories of a lifetime.

We saw some of the most beautiful sights, ate at some of the truck stops we had seen on the Travel Channel. We took a few breaks from the road and saw a few attractions along the way. When we arrived at their place, I was totally exhausted. I laid claim on one of the boy's bed and I slept for a few hours. When I awoke, it was dark out and I was so hungry. Only one of the boys was actually awake. My oldest, we had some quiet time alone and he took me to a restaurant to get something to eat. We sat at the bar and I had a beer with him. I had always told him that I would buy him his first legal drink. Well he turned 21 in a dry country, so this was the soonest I could make good on that promise. I had a really great time with them. I was sad to fly home, after having such a wonderful time with my kids.

A few months later my youngest was homesick, so I purchased a ticket and flew him home. I told him that he was going to be setting himself some goals. And that I wasn't going to ease up until they were accomplished. The first thing I expected of him was getting his GED. And he did it! I was so proud of him! After that things started coming together for him. Girlfriend, car, job, etc. His brother is getting out of the army and starting his education, he too had found a nice girl.

Friendships flourished, I was becoming friends with a lot of people. I was feeling really good about it. I was always being asked to hang out or do this n that. I had been starved for so long to have people to talk to, confide in, do things with. I finally had that. I was on the go with them, quite often. There were three girls that I hung out with a lot and they were all planning a trip to see one of their sisters in West Virginia. I was asked to go. So I did. We all took turns driving. We laughed and had so much fun. We really cut loose that weekend. I made memories that I will never forget. I felt like a kid. We went out to a bar. We drank and danced. I was standing at the bar talking to my friends. And this really cute guy was looking at me and encouraging me to come out on the dance floor. I looked around, just to be sure he was looking at me. I felt kind of silly. He smiled and mouthed, "yes, you!" I felt a freedom that I had never in my life had. We had such a good time. On the way back from our trip, I was hit with such panic, I fell apart. The girls didn't know what to do or what to think. I had never shown that side of me. We were still far enough from home, that we all had time to talk. I revealed things about myself, that they never knew. I was very weak and they gave me strength. Just as close friends should. I didn't want to go back home to the uncomfortable life I was living. I wasn't happy, and that weekend opened my eyes to that. There was more buried deep within and there were issues that I needed to tend to.

Things weren't really going along OK. I was just biding my "time". I had started a friendship with a guy I had known for a long time. We had been friends but we found a connection. There were things that had been said and a look in each others eyes that just drew us together. I trusted him, there was something about him that was special and I was able to confide in him. We really shared a special bond and we were really open with each other. He opened my eyes to so many things about myself. I in turn did the same for him. There were many things that he didn't see, we were becoming very close friends. It was nice to talk to someone. It was nice to have someone look in my eyes and ask me about me. And LISTEN! I was finding confidence I'd never had. He made me realize there was a person inside me and that I was so much more than what I saw in the mirror. I wasn't sure what would come of this friendship, but I knew he would be forever my friend.

One evening at work, in Feb of last year, I was close to being done my shift. And my friend from school that was back in my life, walked in. The look on her face, I will never forget. She took me by the arm, lead me into the bathroom and shut the door. She looked me right in the eyes and said, "listen to me carefully." she took a deep breath, as if to gulp up enough air to give her courage…"your father passed away…" I felt as if my world had come to an end. I lost it, I couldn't keep it together. I fell apart there in the bathroom at work. I cried and cried, I felt as if I had been kicked in the stomach. I'd of taken a beating from my ex husband again, rather than have my dad pass away on me. I was a total basket case. The anxiety was running ramped. I felt as though my world as I knew it had just come to an end, and it had. It was the most horrible feeling. I couldn't believe it, this wasn't happening to me. I thought this must be a dream, come on, pinch me and wake me up from this nightmare. She drove me home or at least what I had called home for the past five plus years. My boyfriend was there, he'd already known the news. I couldn't figure out why he didn't come to work for me. Why was my friend the one that told me? didn't he say he loved me? Why would he let me deal with that news on my own? He held me for a little while and I got agitated. I needed to make some phone calls and leave that house. I couldn't be there, I needed to be gone. My heart was breaking in a way I'd never imagined before. I didn't know how I was going to possibly survive this.

I called my brother and we talked for a bit. Both of us were in shock. Our dad was the most vibrant, and the most alive individual out of the four boys that our grandmother had. They had all had some health issues, except our father. I called my boys and let them know, I told my son I'd contact the Red Cross as soon as I heard more. So he could come home and be here with me. I desperately needed him and his strength.

I grabbed my pills and went to my girl friend's house. I couldn't take being there in that house with him. I went home with her and her family was very welcoming. I was just beside myself. In shock. I was so drained and it had just begun. My new found best friend called me and came to see me. He had heard the news. I hugged him and held on for dear life. He cared more for me than that man back at that house. I felt that all there in that instant. He went out of his way to be with me and hold me. I will forever be grateful for his love. I realized that I was lucky to have best friends and they were all around me.

I took a few pills that night to calm the anxiety and be able to relax and sleep. Life as I knew it, had just ended. In that one event, so many things came to realization. I knew I wasn't happy where I was at and I knew that I had to make a change. I didn't know how or when, but I did know that in that moment, that night I lost my father.

My dad was so full of life. He laughed and worked hard. He put his *ALL* into everything he did. He was a wonderful caring, kind man. There were so many things that went, UN - said, that scared me. There were so many things that I should have told him. I was terrified that he didn't know what he meant to me. He was the first person that I had lost, that was that close to me. Besides the summer that his mother, my grandmother died, the year my oldest son was born. Life is too short to live it unhappily and my dad proved that to me.

I finally spoke to my step mother. I knew my dad would've wanted me there for her. With my brother being out of state I was the one that needed to step it up. She had her family too, siblings. Her and my father never had kids, so to her, my brother & I were her's too.

My best friend went with us to the funeral home. That was very emotional. I hadn't ever had that to deal with. The man we dealt with there was quite experienced and made the decisions easy. Arrangements were made so that the immediate family could say good bye. Me being the biggest reason it was for. Funny how life deals you little gifts, for once a decision that involved others, was all about me. This was something that my step mother was wanting for me. It had been some time, since I had seen my dad. Being that it was winter and the job he had, he was very busy plowing the roads. He went to bed early, and arose during the night to see what the weather was doing.

My son came home and he spent a lot of time with me. This trip home was for mom. The boys weren't too close to their grandfather and I regretted that very much. The passing affected them still, they were pretty upset and they saw how it was affecting me. It was the very first time they experienced a loss that close, as well. Seeing my father displayed there in that funeral home, was not an easy sight, that sure wasn't the vibrant person that they knew. It was even harder on me. I was saying good bye to my hero. I remember thinking, aren't super-heroes invincible? He was someone I looked up to. Someone I'd always admired & loved very deeply. An era of my life had come to a close. I kissed him on his forehead and I brushed his beautiful gray locks of hair back. I whispered "I love you daddy" and "good bye, until we meet again...". I just stood back and looked at him. Knowing that it was indeed the last time I would see him, I had great difficulty leaving. It was right there in front of me, but I still couldn't believe it. The reality of it was still not in me, I was just waiting for him to sit up and scare me, and laugh that mischievous laugh that I loved so much. But it didn't happen...I stood there staring at him for the longest time. Thinking. Thinking of all the things that I should have said to him, all the things that I wish I had done. So many regrets, if I had allowed it, it would drive me insane. Seeing him there was so surreal, he had always been active, full of life. He worked hard and only gave things his very best effort. And now, he was resting...

He was being cremated and the memorial service was scheduled for about a month away. We all had time to reflect and let the pain of losing him sink in. My brother was coming home and he was a lot of my strength. He and I had become distant, a few years before and lost touch. But all in that one night of tragedy, we buried it all. Dad had brought us back together. We got through the memorial service, clinging pretty close to each other. The town had allowed my dad's favorite piece of equipment to be displayed in front of the church. His crew washed it up and made it shine, they took great care of it. The grader that he loved so much was there at the church to say good bye to it's beloved operator. My dad's road crew was there, it was just two younger boys. They were pretty upset and they were right there the whole time. Helping where it was needed and they seemed to be hanging on as long as they could as well. It was touching to see them, they loved him too. He was truly more than just my hero, others felt the same way.

Since he passed away in the winter, a service was planned for summer just after his birthday. The National Guard was going to do their dedication & send him "off" with the respect that was due.

Now that the memorial service was over and that part of my life was closed until summer. I moved on with getting my life in order. I was battling with so many things. Death. My father and the man I'd been living with. From that night of my dad's passing, I was never to see the place I called home for five years, as home - ever again. My heart was gone from there long before and with my father's passing, it was time to move on.

My best friend that was always there for me, throughout this tragedy, was allowing me to stay at her house. Her daughters were a great source of love and smiles. I will be forever thankful for the love that was given to me there.

So one evening we went to my dad's house, I will forever see it as that. It was something that he built, it is just such a serene place to be. I was dreading being there, and I was excited to be there. Every where I look, I see my father, the dread was that he was no longer there. We spent the evening with my step mother. We laughed, we cried, we drank wine. We talked about dad and his values, his quirks, his work and his love. My father spoke to me through her that night. She gave me the answer I'd been battling with. My dad never thought I should be with the guy I was with. He didn't like him. My best friend's eyes met mine, each of us full of tears, she heard him speak just as I had. She knew what it meant to me. It just confirmed what was in my heart and it sealed my decision. She went on to tell me more that night. She told me things that I had so desired and been starved to hear for so many years. She told me that he was never disappointed in me, he was so proud of me. To him, I could do no wrong. Those words hit me to my very core. They were words that I needed to hear so many times, and in death is how I got them. He spoke to me through her in so many ways that night. I was her connection to him and she was mine.

I went and told this guy that I was moving out and it was over. He didn't like it. I was trying to be gentle. I tried for a long time. It went on for months, he was still holding on to hope that I would come back. He even went and bought a ring, and wanted me to marry him. I was livid! I wasn't good enough back when I asked, I am not good enough now. I was hurt even more that he wanted to marry me then. Are you kidding me? No way would I marry someone that had no problem trampling on my heart when I opened it up to him.

A few months passed. I was hanging out with my new guy friend pretty steady. I had actually fallen in love with him. He was my best friend. We were becoming extremely close. We couldn't go a day without seeing each other. He was the one person in my life that made me happy. I could talk to him, tell him anything. Fears, joys, dreams, hopes and just be myself. That feeling was incredible.

My mother called me in a panic one Saturday afternoon. I had never before heard that despair in her voice. Her husband had had a stoke. So I got to her as fast as I could and took her to him. It was bad. He'd been pretty sick over the past ten years. There was no turning back from this stroke. He was in the IC Unit for a week. There was a living will in place and he wanted to be taken off life support if it was ever that bad. So he was...They moved him to a private room and made him comfortable. He would open his eyes, but when you looked in them, they were hollow and he wasn't there. He held on for his daughter to get there from out of state. Her brother had been there through it all. A few hours after she arrived, he took his last breath. Surrounded by his wife of 22 years and his kids.

Another death. In a two month span. I called the funeral home, having dealt with them not so long before. I got the ball rolling on that. I committed to taking care of my mom. We had never been close. I'd always wanted it, but it wasn't there. My ex husband, her husband, there were many factors involved. But my mother needed me now. And I was stepping it up. She had me move in with her, so that she wasn't alone.

I couldn't believe how life was turning out. I was coming full circle. Moving back into the house that I had grown up in. All because of death hitting home twice within months! Both couples had been together for more than twenty years. It really made me take a second look at my life. So here I was, me & my dog. Moved into my mother's house. Sleeping in the room that I'd grown up in. Sharing a house with the woman that gave birth to me and had been so distant from because of life. Because of our spouses...I know she had had it hard. Her life up to that point had not been a bowl of cherries either. Her & I shared a lot. Pain and a difficult life. We both had a great deal of pain to come to terms with along with our grieving. So our recovery began. We went shopping, went out to dinner, we drank wine and giggled till late into the night. We found the start of something that was well deserved. A mother daughter friendship. We were both losing weight and needed new clothes. We started talking and I found my mother, a companion I'd longed for. With two deaths, I was given that gift.

In July, we had the funeral service for my father. One last good bye. My brother came home alone this time and stayed with mom and I. Which was a healing thing for them as well. We'd all distanced ourselves from one another and we were coming together. They talked and it was really good.

Back in Feb when we were planning the memorial for dad, I made sure that someone from the armed forces would be there at the cemetery. The service was small and we sat under that tent looking at the hole in the ground. My brother and I in that front row, closest to that hole that was dug, just for that little box of ashes in which I knew as my dad. We sat together crying, tears that had been built up for him. Reflecting on so many things. Little did I know, I would be the one presented with the flag. That representative of the Army National Guard, knelt in front of me, not batting an eye, started his speech. "On behalf of the President of the United States..." word for word, just as I had seen it done in the movies and on tv. I was so touched, so emotional. So many things reeled through my mind at that moment. My father, my son, the creed of a soldier. This soldier kneeling in front of me, didn't personally know my dad and how wonderful a man he was. But he was saying those words to me, he was looking into my eyes as they welled up with tears for the man I love so much. I wanted so much at that very moment, to wake up, it had to be a dream, a really bad dream. I wanted to scream, I wanted to say NO, this isn't true, this isn't real. I still couldn't believe he was gone, even though it was right in front of me. Regrets. So many regrets. I'd realized that I couldn't do it any more. I could not live with regrets. I had to bury them there that day, in the cemetery. My dad wouldn't have wanted me to regret, he would have wanted me to learn. So I told myself, NO MORE REGRETS!!

The visit that we had with my brother was really good. He invited mom & I down to visit him and his family in Florida. We said that we would. Little did I know, mom's wheels were turning. Within weeks we were planning a trip for after the holidays. Florida seemed to be the place to go to refresh yourself. I went after my huge struggle and now mom was going after her's. While he was home this time we went to dad's house to see our step mother. Find some closure on some of that we had just gone through. We had buried only half of dad's ashes at the cemetery that day. The rest was to be scattered about the perimeter of land our father owned and along the woods that surrounded it. The three of us walked throughout the property, each of us taking a hand full of dad and leaving pieces every where for him to enjoy. We talked and reminisced about dad, the fond memories we had, funny moments we had shared, and the hobbies he had. The quirks he possessed and the things that he got a kick out of, and how often we thought he had a twisted sense of humor. We laughed and we cried. It was sealing the good bye and fair well, so long, until we meet again. Tears of joy for the life that he was blessed to have lived, for the memories and values he gave us. Tears of sorrow for the heart break we were experiencing and knew we would experience for the rest of our days. As we were wrapping our ritual up, our step mother turned and asked if either of us would like some of dad's ashes. It hadn't even occurred to me. Of course I jumped at that opportunity. It made me cry, tears of being touched by the gesture and tears of sorrow, because that was all I had left of him. That was a good day, despite the reason for being there...

Meanwhile, my ex boyfriend was still coming around. I was grateful for the help he gave my mother. Some things need to be done by a man and he was there to help. He was becoming a good friend to her. Despite the uncomfortable feeling I had, it was a good thing for her. And at that point, it was about my mom. I was there to help her, not hinder her.

Towards the end of July, my friend that had got my ex husband and I together was planning a trip to Maine to visit one of our other friends from our childhood. She asked me to go. I was tickled pink. She was going for the week, I couldn't get out of work. So I left right from work Friday evening. I drove to Maine at 8:00 at night, all by myself. I knew that I had the wings to do it. I was nervous about it, but I did it! I had the freedom. I had the strength. I had the desire to get out on my own and do more. This was my opportunity to prove something to myself. I did it. I stayed the whole weekend. I had a really good time. It was so awesome to be with the two friends that I had hung out with so much, many years before. It felt like old times. It felt really good to see her and her kids. I left early that Sunday morning. I was planning on making a trip to Portland to see the lighthouse. I drove through and explored the town. I found the lighthouse, and I stayed and took many pictures. It was a beautiful, warm and sunny day. With a gentle summer wind coming off the coast. I enjoyed the view for what seemed like hours. Reflecting on what it meant to me to be there. My father had always loved Maine, and in some strange way that day, I felt closer to him just being there. Standing by that lighthouse, knowing what the job of a lighthouse is. A beacon of light to guide a ship in the night. It felt as if that was what it was doing for me as well.

    I continued seeing my guy friend. We had got so close over the months. I felt as if I couldn't live a day without seeing him. I got butterflies in my stomach, just thinking about him. I gave him tickets to a baseball game in NYC for his birthday. So we planned a trip. A trip that I will treasure forever. We fell even more in love, I had no idea that life could be so good. So joyous, so happy. I felt as if I was on a honey moon trip. I felt as if I were the star of a movie. That is how perfect it was. It felt real, it felt comfortable, it felt secure and it felt like it was meant to be. I had never in my life experienced the feelings that I did that weekend we went away. We learned so much about each other. We talked, we dined at a nice restaurant, we got lost in the Bronx. Neither of us nervous or worried about not knowing where we were. We were together and that was all that we needed. We discovered what a great team we are together. He drove and I ran the GPS, improvising, giggling, and sitting in traffic. We had so much fun.

    After the holidays mom and I went to Florida. She hadn't been on a trip like that, ever. She was nervous but very excited about it all. I felt like the mother at times, watching her. She was overwhelmed a few times with what to do at the airport. I was the seasoned traveler and knew what to do. We arrived late into Orlando and I had written the directions down from my brother. Well I forgot one important element when I was jotting it down. A ride that should have taken half an hour, took us a few hours. We laughed and giggled like school girls, we cranked the radio and sang along at times. Spontaneously I busted out into a dance, I have never seen my mother laugh so hard. She had found a new saying that she really liked. "Sometimes I laugh so hard, the tears run down my leg", I think she found that happening. We arrived at our motel about 1am. We were tired. We were giddy. We didn't get to sleep until about 4am, we were just so excited to be there.

    We went to my brother's the next morning. After just a few hours of sleep, we were ready to go and get on with our vacation. We were greeted with open arms and it was really great to see all three of them. My niece had grown like a weed and she was more beautiful than I had remembered her. She hadn't forgot me. She was wearing a necklace that I had sent to her for Christmas. We did so many things that week. We were able to spend a few days with all three of them, my brother, his wife and my niece. We went to both sides of the state so we could say we had been to both bodies of water. I walked in the sand and stuck my feet in the salty ocean water. It was so relaxing being there. The weather was gorgeous. We went and saw the manatees at a park nearby. We went to the Universal City Walk and drank margaritas at Jimmy Buffet's Margaritaville. We went shopping. We walked a lot and just enjoyed seeing everything there was to do.

    One day mom was able to go with my brother to work. He owns his own tractor trailer and she rode along for the day. That was a really good thing for them. They talked like they had never talked before. It really brought them closer and their healing began on that day.

There were a few days that it was mom, my brother and I. Just the three of us. That, we were never able to do often. We had such a good time. My brother and I were in the front when we drove anywhere and stuffed mom in the back. We giggled and picked on her. We would be talking away and she only heard bits of the conversation. She was quite a tourist in the back seat with her camera. We were pretty amused with that. It was rather cute.

One of the days, the three of us went to Daytona Beach. We drove out on the beach and then parked the car. We walked and walked. Enjoyed the sun and surf, dipped our toes in the water. Basked in the serene sounds of the ocean and found seashells. We stopped by Daytona Speedway just to look around and walked the Daytona 500 Walk of Fame. As we were driving out of town, my brother and I spotted something. A go-cart track. I cranked the wheel and we were going! This was a day to feel like a kid again and we were going to live it up. We were the only ones there at that time of day, the track was ours. I haven't seen my brother smile like that in years. We raced each other and laughed and laughed. I think that day with my brother was my favorite. We all bonded on that trip. There was healing and a closeness that had never been present. The whole trip was a gift. My mother discovered her wings, she ruffled her feathers. She knew they were always there, just as I had my own. She expanded her horizons, her eyes were opened to more than just a vacation. She was healing from years of hurt and the recent loss.

Back on that evening that my best friend and I went to see my step mother, not long after my dad's passing. She revealed to me that my dad wanted me to go to Florida on a trip to see my brother with him. We just never got to it. If I had known, I would have jumped on that opportunity. Being that it never happened. The morning that we were leaving for the airport, I took a piece of my dad with me. I put some of his ashes in a container and he was making that trip that he wanted. When I was putting those ashes into the container, there was an image that they made. There was a perfect image of angel wings. I knew what I was doing would have been silly to most. But I wanted my dad to go on that trip. When I saw those wings form in those ashes, I knew I was doing something special for him. I cried, tears of sadness, but mostly tears of joy. I felt like I was able to give my dad something, a gift. Looking back now, it was very special. Only, one from a divorced family would appreciate this gift. The four of us were together. My dad, my mom, my brother and I. Silly or not, that was what I dreamed of when I was younger. Every kid wants their family together, and for one week, in a weird way, I got that.

Being away for a week really made me realize a lot. I had discovered that I had never been in love up to that point in my life! For the first time ever, I was head over heels in love. I couldn't stand being away from him. I missed him so much, my heart ached to be back in his arms. He is such a wonderful man, a good man. He builds me up. He treats me with respect. He listens to what I say. He asks me my opinion. He encourages me. He loves me unconditionally. These are all things that I have never been blessed with and now I have! All I do is think about him. He's in my every waking moment. I long to be with him when we are apart. When we are together, I miss him all ready, just in anticipation of being apart. I have never loved, until I found this true love. A love of a lifetime. I have found my soul mate. I am not letting this go, I am holding on for dear life. Because life has become so dear to me.

The turn of events in my life over the past few years, have forever changed me. I will never look at life the way I used to. If life is to get better, how does it happen without change? Something has to improve in order for there to be change. You need to have courage to step out of your comfort zone. With each little step you take, comes more confidence. It will come. Just trust in yourself. Know that you are more than you see in the mirror.

I have the love of a man that has forever changed me. In my father's death, it brought him closer to me. He was the rock that I could lean on. He opened my eyes to so many things I had never seen. I will be forever grateful for his love. To love someone and say that you have learned from that love, is a treasured gift. If there were no results in the happily ever after, don't look at it as wasted time. If you were really, deeply in love and there were circumstances beyond your control as to why you aren't together. Try not to be heartbroken, although, much easier said than done. Keep the memories and that feeling of being in love, in your heart, remember every detail. Don't take it for granted. Embrace it when it is given, it is a gift not given freely and not just to anyone. You vested in a precious commodity. Yourself and the love. If you have loved, you have lived. I have learned so much. Life lessons are way more valuable than a college degree.

Life is certainly not perfect, we all make mistakes, have victories. We may not all be lucky enough to find that perfect person, a soul mate. I believe that Fate does put people in your path for a reason. I believe you know, when you find that person. You feel it in your whole being, in your heart. You ache when you are apart. Feel blessed to have known that feeling, if you are one of the lucky ones to have found it. There is no replacing it. There is only one. If you aren't able to hold it and keep it, remember what it felt like. Cherish every single minute you have shared. Feel like the luckiest person in the world, because you are. Some live all their lives not ever knowing that truly happy, blissful feeling. Once they are gone, they never will.

So if you are one of those that have found your soul mate and are with that mate every day... YOU ARE BLESSED! YOU HAVE "WON THE LOTTERY"!!! Live each day with that person and cherish them. Do not let anything stand in your way. Always hold hands, always kiss when parting, always say I love you, you never know when you will be able to say it again.

I now have confidence. I now walk knowing I can do anything I want. I keep my hair the way I want it, short. I wear make up everyday. I buy the perfume I like to wear because I know that I'm worth it. I have a closet full of clothes that I bought and I wear. I wear high heels. I wear sandals that are open toed, I was never allowed to when I was married. I can wear a low cut shirt or a short skirt, and do it with freedom. I was before, called names when I tried to wear something that was a little revealing. I feel good about myself. I could stand to lose more weight, but I am comfortable. I have transformed into the woman that was stuck inside this abused and battered body. That woman within is shining through, just as a lighthouse.

I have learned more about myself in the past few months. Some things have just fallen into place, unexpected things. For the very first time in my life, I am out on my own. I was very skeptical about taking the plunge into the unknown all alone. My mother was taking the same steps I was. She had never been alone on her own either. We were walking a new path together. She helping me and I helping her. Discovering more about each other. Fearing that the bond we shared, be broken by moving out of the house I'd thought of as home. She has spread her wings, yet again. Finding out just how far she can soar. I too have discovered that feeling. Independence. Freedom. Being you...Something that neither one of us have had, but now cherish. My mother smiles and is very happy, despite me leaving her nest. I too have spread my wings and found the freedom of soaring. The tranquil flight of being out on your own is very rewarding. For some, that has always been the way of life. I never could understand how they did it, I was so envious. Now I know that feeling, and hope those around me that I have known out on their own, realize how special they have had life.

I am so blessed to have found the apartment I have. I am able to keep my lifetime companion, my baby, Shih Tzu. I have been to yard sales, flea markets, craigslist & thrift stores, you can find so many treasures. It doesn't have to be perfect, sometimes used is better. I have turned a bland white walled apartment, into my sanctuary. I have the freedom to put a picture where I want it. If I choose to sleep on the futon instead of my bed, I CAN! You really don't know what you are capable of until a door of opportunity is opened. You sometimes have to make it open, give the door a little kick and don't be afraid of failing. What is life if you don't take a chance? Are you ever going to know, if you don't leap? Leap into the faith that has grown in you. You don't know, if you don't try. Change can be scarey, change can be intimidating. But change is good.

I have been living away from my mother for about six months now. I go by her house on my way to work, so the two different roofs over our heads have not changed what we share. It's actually made us closer. We plan on coffee some mornings and we plan on a few beers after a long week at work. I have even spent the night in my old bed, just because I'd had a few too many. We laugh and we talk. We remember and scheme up new memories. But most of all, we are there for each other as never before. When I step back and think of how far we have traveled and the trip it took to get there...The thought is filled with sorrow and happiness. Sorrow for all the years lost. Happiness for all the years we hope are ahead.

Amazing things happen when you have friends. I had truly forgot that and what it feels like. I was recently blessed with a girl's weekend. Two friends I grew up with and a new one I just met on this trip. Primary one being the friend that was always there for me growing up, the one that I was hanging out with the night I met my ex husband. She used to be such a major part of my life. With my abusive marriage, she was pushed away. Day to day life was all about my two boys and surviving. Anticipating what the next struggle would be. I allowed her to be pushed away to protect her.

About five years ago we reconnected, thanks to her calling on me. We have slowly getting back to what we once had. It certainly doesn't mend itself over night. For many years she thought that she had done something wrong. I allowed it to happen, I didn't want her to see what I was going through and I also wanted to protect her. After not having friends in my life for so many years, I have realized that I need to re – learn the fundamentals of being a friend and how to nurture those relationships.

 We'd planned on this girl's weekend for a few months. As it got closer, I wasn't sure I'd be able to go. Just because of money. Being out on my own now, I look at money differently, as I should. I put aside an "x" amount of money and as it arrived on us, I said, "I have to go!!" We need to do this. There are some things in life that you just owe yourself, and this was indeed one of those things. So I went, we were totally spontaneous. We planned a destination and when we got there, everything was shut down, the season was done. We bounced some ideas out and ended up in Atlantic City. So exciting! So much to do and so much to see. Still had the beach, shopping and a bonus, casino's! Never had the desire before, but I soon got into it. I learned a lot about "old" friends and I made a new friend. It was a well deserved treat.

 A few weeks following, I was able to reunite two people. Two people that mean a lot to me. Two people that hadn't spoken in over twenty years. Both of my best friends from grade school. We were inseparable at one time in our lives. We had so much fun, laughing and remembering so many things. The three of us had spent so much time together and we had a lot of catching up to do. Just watching their faces as they talked was hysterical, they discovered how much they missed each other. We then looked at old photos, we found so many that brought back memories. We found one of the three of us – smiling and NOT looking any different, well maybe younger and innocent. Now we are wiser. In one evening, I ignited a spark in two friends that have been apart for far too long. We all agreed to do it again. Hopefully they will never be absent in each others lives again, and hopefully always in my life as well.

 As these quality times with friends have been spent in the past few weeks, I have really reflected. Reflected on regrets and remembering I buried those in the cemetery with part of my Dad. Reflected on what an abusive man did to me. He stole so much from me. Years that I will never get back, years with friends, years of seeing them. Years of seeing their kids be born & grow up. I know them all now, teenagers, but so many years lost. But...no more regrets. We are moving on, pressing on, making new memories, nurturing the broken hearts and making up for lost time. We will see the grand children, we will help each other cover up the gray highlights that we have earned. When one of us needs a new hip, we will be there to bring them flowers and put hot pink polish on their toes...

 Forty years have come and gone, we hope for another forty. We're closing a book in our lives and pressing on to the next part of the trilogy they call life.

 I have a love for the ocean and lighthouses. I've always known why the ocean is so appealing to me. It's the calming sounds of the waves, the seagulls singing, the sand in between my toes... I have had such turmoil, it has been a very tranquil place for me to be. I can sit there and have my own thoughts. I can take a "break" from the world around me. It is my dreamland. It wasn't until this very morning that I figured out the fascination with the lighthouses. You may think they go hand in hand. But there has always been something very special to me about a lighthouse. I may have said it before, I'm not sure. But it really struck me hard today. They come in so many colors, different shapes, and several locations. They sit on the edge of the land. They weather many storms, and they still stand. They may have paint chipped and stones out of place. Ghosts haunting the stairway to the light at the top. So they are flawed. They aren't perfect. But they still serve their purpose. They still stand there, they still guide ships in the night, in the fog, when it's not clear. They are very strong structures. I see more in that lighthouse than it's beauty, it's flaws. I see a structure that is unstoppable, indestructible, resilient, encouraged and strong. I AM A LIGHTHOUSE!! I have been through the experiences of a lighthouse. I've been stressed under pressure. I have weathered many storms, I have been beaten up and battered. I have shone my light through the dark. I am strong and resilient. There is beauty in all lighthouses, whether they are rusted and not so attractive to the eye OR if they have a fresh coat of paint and beautiful landscaping. They are all gorgeous, just as human beings... So the next time you see a lighthouse, stop, admire the beauty with enlightened eyes, hearts, mind & soul. Be a beacon, a light for others to follow.

My journey isn't over. There will be more pain. There will be more joy and happiness. I have survived. I have over come. I have fled from a monster and I am still here. I know my father would be proud of his little girl. He taught me and gave me so much. Not only while he was living but in his death as well. He woke me up, so I could smell the roses. So I could appreciate the things that don't cost a dime. Cherish the gifts that are given, even when there is death involved. Cherish what and who I have in my life. The relationships that have flourished. The relationships that have been given life. The gift of family is so precious.

This isn't the end. This is a closing of a book in my life. The story does continue. My life is just beginning. I have learned many lessons, some difficult and some joyous. I have been trampled on and stepped on. I have triumphed and had victory. Days of being near death and days so happy, I thought I would burst. Days of being so high on life, I was floating in the clouds. There was a time I would've dwelled on the past and been so low & depressed. Thinking about the troubles I've had and I would've not moved on in my life. Now I look back on it all and I think about how far I have come. I'm still up right. I'm still here. I'm still making memories to cherish in my heart forever. I now have my mother in my life. I have my brother and his family, that I treasure. I have the friends that I longed for, for so long. I have my dog that lightens my days and makes me smile. I have the love of a man like no other. And most of all I have my two boys.

I held onto so much hurt for so long. I know I can go on. I know I will never go back to what I once was. I was a battered woman. I was a victim of domestic violence. I was abused mentally and physically. No more. I am so much more than the reflection I see in the mirror. I know I have a lot to offer the world. And I know that if I can give someone the strength and knowledge to know what they are going through is wrong, and save one person's life. Then it was all worth the years I struggled.

I have truly come full circle. I am living the second part of my life. I live in my hometown. I drive by my dad's workplace, I see all of the wooden signs he made, marking the roads in the town he loved so much. I drive by the school I went to every day, I remember some of the school lunches. We had a really good cook. I drive by the general store, remembering how I worked there, one of my first jobs. I remember... Almost two years ago I couldn't have said that. I had blocked out many memories. As I started jotting down notes for this book and went through therapy for about six months, I started remembering things that I had forgot. Some understandable, some not. Like riding with a friend to the school dances, her dad taking us and being goofy. Slamming on the brakes, just to see "that spider cross the road..." Fun memories. Good memories. Treasured memories. I am making more memories with those friends that I grew up with, I am making new friends.

This was my story, it's not over. I am pressing on, everyday I find strength I never knew was there. Every day is a new adventure for me. Every day I get out of bed, hoping to learn something new. I look back and see what I have been through. I know that I have had it a lot worse. I know that I will get through whatever struggles I have. Some days may not be perfect, but I do carry on, knowing that tomorrow is another day. Reflect on what I learned... I'm not sure what my future holds. That I take one step at a time. But I do know that what I have learned and what I remember, shapes the person that I am today. I haven't shared my story for sympathy. I don't want you to feel sorry for me. I want to enrich other people's lives and give encouragement to others. Show them how things can work, what is possible, and to not loose hope, because not all hope is lost!

A friend that I have known since grade school found out some of the details of my life. Things that she had never known. She cried and said she felt bad that she wasn't there for me. I told her not to feel bad! It is what it is. I am here. I am standing. What has happened to me has made me the person that I am today. Don't feel bad for me, I don't want sympathy. I want you to know what I have been through, I want you to be proud of me for the journey I have traveled and the stories that I can now share. It wasn't all for nothing, I have conquered the rough waters. I am finally starting to sail out to sea, calm, and tranquilly.

I will have victory. I will be strong. I will fight and never go back to what once was. Because I am strong. I am confident. I am free. I am not perfect. I do strive to be better. I am a friend. I am a mother. I am a daughter. I am encouraged. I am ME. I am a light, watch me shine. I hope I am a hero to someone. I am no longer silent and that is the truth.

And just remember this, every day that goes by, is one that you will never get back.

**The truth is no longer silent...**

Hold me close and say you love me,
then you go and push and shove me!
What have I done, what did I do?
If people just really knew,
that would be the end of you!
You lie and cheat and hold your head
up high,
please god just make him die!
I am better you just can't take it,
my damn arm you try to break.
But guess what jerk I'm still standing!
On my feet I am landing!
Looking back I have to wonder,
who it was that stole your thunder?
A petty man with no honor,
hit a man and you would be a goner!
Guess what I'm still here,
someday it will be me you fear!

Please visit my website. Type in dealingwithviolence

Please give to the Red Cross, they are one of those really worthy causes!

And please think about giving to your local shelters. There are so many places that can use your old sheets and blankets, warm coats and gloves. Look up your local state agency, the shelters are not for the public to know where they are located. That is to protect the victims of crime. If you know someone or are a victim yourself. Make a plan to get out, you are worth it. You do count. There are resources out there in every single state, that can help you break away. I found this info out just recently. If I had known that information fifteen years ago...my life would have been different.

After thoughts...

The affects of PTSD go on – repressed memories still find their way back into my daily life. An image I see, a pain I feel, a smell that touches my nose...anything can trigger it. Anything to this day, the memories can be crippling. I guess it's all in how I deal with these demons, that determines my survival. I can go weeks and even months with no recollections. But then out of the blue comes something new. I am stronger than I once was. I am human.

Not all the memories that come back are bad. Sitting on the couch the other night, snuggling up to watch a movie. My dog beside me, ruffling up a big comforter a memory came back to me. A simple sweet memory...when my brother & I were little, just home from school watching cartoons or home with the chick pox, laying on the couch. I remember being snuggled up my "puff" (comforter) and playing matchbox cars on top of the "puff". We each had our own collections, mine was in a big cosmetic case my grandmother had given me. We would ruffle up the blankets and create mountains and cool roads to drive the cars on. Just a nice memory from my childhood that came back to me, just by looking down and seeing a wrinkle in my comforter...which reeled into another.

When we were kids we loved to play with Tonka trucks, they don't make them like that any more. But Dad saw the love we shared for the trucks and he got a load of sand delivered to the house. We spent hours and hours out there playing in that pile of dirt. The noises my brother made, mimicking the sound of a "jake brake", the excelling sound of a big truck and the growl of bucket loader working. Thinking back now, he has done in his adulthood, what he played in our backyard. He is one of those lucky ones that followed his dream. Instead of playing those sounds, he puts the big pipes on his big KW to make it louder. He takes his mother and sister with him in the tractor trailer, sharing his love of big equipment. Allowing us to see what a wonderful craftsman he is behind that big wheel. Reminding me of the song we used to listen to over and over again. Roll on, by Alabama, the rev of the engine in the beginning of that song, we used to rewind and rewind the tape just to hear it. Now he listens to the purr of the motor every day when he goes to work. I'm so proud of him!

Memories do still bother me. Tears still flow, with the after effects of domestic abuse. How I deal with it is the key. Some days I feel like I fail, but I stop and remember how far I have come. I may be forty years old, but I still learn everyday. It makes me strive for better and fuels my passion to stop domestic violence. It fuels the desire I have for a brighter future. I want no woman, man or child to live in fear. It's no way to live. It isn't living. It's a prison, with a death sentence, not knowing when the electric chair will be fired up & primed to be used. The fear of not knowing when your last day on Earth will be...Scared of the unknown and what may greet you at the door when you arrive to that place you call *HOME*. But it's not home, it has bars on the windows, that only you can see. Living that life day after day, when you haven't committed a crime, is criminal. That person that is keeping you hostage & walking on pins and needles is criminal. They need to be stopped. You need to take control back, step away from that "comfort zone" and take control of yourself. Make that escape and get out. You have to stop the cycle. That little two year old boy will grow up seeing and thinking that this is normal. AND IT ISN'T!! Love yourself & your child enough to say, THIS IS ENOUGH! Stop the violence, bring an end to the silence. You have a responsibility to raise that little boy right. Even if you have to struggle or swallow your pride, it is way better than struggling to survive. Look into that precious little face – that is the future. That my dear, is a future abuser or a future victim. THAT IS THE REALITY...

The past is what defines you as a person today. Embrace it, confront it & learn from it. For it is the past & move on to a brighter future. Because the ones of the past are in the past, you can control them being in your future. That is indeed a way to love yourself.

This book was a long, difficult journey for me to travel. But I have done it. That is the truth and it's no longer silent.

Printed in Great Britain
by Amazon